Hope Bourne's
EXMOOR VILLAGE

Hope Bourne's
EXMOOR VILLAGE

HOPE L. BOURNE

Illustrations by the author

HALSGROVE

First published in 2015
Reprinted in 2017

ISBN 978 0 85704 256 9

British Library Cataloguing-in-Publication-Data
A CIP data for this book is available from the British Library

HALSGROVE
Halsgrove House,
Ryelands Business Park,
Bagley Road, Wellington, Somerset TA21 9PZ
Tel: 01823 653777 Fax: 01823 216796
email: sales@halsgrove.com

Part of the Halsgrove group of companies
Information on all Halsgrove titles is available at:
www.halsgrove.com

Printed and bound in India by Parksons Graphics

CONTENTS

H.S.L.B. 1954

Preface

For many years now Withypool under the long shadow of the moor has been my home. I have lived in first one and then another of the isolated spots in the parish, and now, latterly, I have lived in the village itself. Up to a few years ago, however, leading a very active life, I spent much of my time outside of the parish, walking or riding, following the hounds, camping out, staying with friends at lonely farms, ranging in general over the length and breadth of Exmoor and daily exploring all the high windy spaces, hidden combes, and tangled woods of this lovely land. My own particular nook of country I rather took for granted in the context of the whole, and came and went from my own little cottage here.

Then, just about three years ago from this time of writing, I sustained a complete breakdown, due to certain very great personal unhappiness, and upon recovery found myself, for the time being at least, quite unable to continue in the same way of life – in short, I no longer had the extreme physical strength and vigour that had previously been mine.

So, perforce, I came to spend most of my time pottering in my garden and around the bits of country immediately to hand, my wanderings circumscribed by the brief mile or so that I could now walk in a day. Gradually I began to realise two things: how much I loved this place, this district, in which every field and every tree, every stream and every bit of rough moor, had become known and dear to me, every scrap of it holding some memory or association; and also, more impersonally, how Withypool itself was set into the midst of the moorland country so that a mile's walk in any direction would bring one to hills, woods and combes as lovely as any upon the whole of Exmoor. I began to realise also how fortunate I was to live in Withypool, with all the many aspects of the moor here right to hand, almost on my doorstep as it were. I know of no other place where one may have everything in so small a compass.

Gradually a desire was born to write something about this, my own place, to make some offering to it. The feeling grew that even as it was my home, and I belonged here, so I owed it allegiance and some offering. So I began to write this little book.

What I have written here is what I know of Withypool and what its nooks and corners have meant to me. It is not all that there is to tell of

Withypool, for there is much more to be delved into and recorded, and probably many ancient documents to be studied by anyone who has the time and inclination and interest in the past, but, as I have said, it is what I know personally of this moorland parish which is my home.

Here, then, is my salute to Withypool, a village of the moor in the county of Somerset.

H. L. B.
January, 1970.

Introduction

Hope Lilian Bourne (1918-2010) was born in Oxford towards the end of the Great War. In retrospect, she often seems to have lived on the margins. Her father was a soldier stationed briefly in England and her mother took his surname. However, the exact nature of their relationship is unclear and Hope was brought up by her mother alone. This hint of illegitimacy, of being just outside of social acceptance, runs through Hope's life. Whilst she was aware of social strictures, Hope's lifestyle was often at odds with them.

Hope's mother died in 1953 leaving Hope, in her own words "with no home, no income, and no profession whereby I could earn one".[1] By this time resident on Exmoor, she lived in a succession of semi-derelict cottages until in 1970 she moved to a caravan at Ferny Ball, near Withypool. There she remained until 1994 when she moved into a bungalow in the village. She scraped by, often with no electricity, no bathroom and no running water. She survived by growing her own food, hunting and exchanging labour for meals.

In the 1970s and 1980s Hope rose to prominence as the "Woman of Exmoor". Her lifestyle, which she was at pains to point out was forced on her rather than chosen, became appealing at a time when audiences were entranced by the BBC's *Good Life*. Hope's existence had none of the safety nets available to Tom and Barbara Good but her writings on Exmoor as well as newspaper coverage and television appearances gave her for a time a source of income. It did not last and Hope's correspondence with the publisher Victor Bonham-Carter shows how hand-to-mouth her existence was.

Hope's deep sense of connection with Exmoor was expressed through her writing and her art. She was also prepared to fight to maintain Exmoor as a relatively wild space. Hers is one of the first names on a 1958 petition to stop the afforestation of the Chains, a remote part of the moor. Despite her lack of funds, the first edition of the *Exmoor Review* in 1959 lists her as a five-shilling subscriber to the Exmoor Society. She remained a supporter until her death and in 2010 she left her entire estate to the Society.

Given the array of papers by that time accumulated in the Society's old offices in Dulverton, including Hope's sketches, manuscripts and letters, the Society decided to employ a full-time archivist. I was appointed to the post in March 2014. As a preliminary survey of the material I dug through various old boxes, including one labelled "Village Surveys". There, in two orange cardboard folders, was Hope's Withypool manuscript. Going through her correspondence with Bonham-Carter I was able to trace the manuscript's history. Hope had written it in the winter of 1969 and presented it to Bonham-Carter for publication. He rejected it on the grounds that it "suffers from the faults of so many local histories, having long 'pedestrian' pieces in it".[2] However, he did pay to have it typed up, at a cost of £44 4s and 6d. Once the typescript was returned to Hope she edited it and added passages. She then deposited it in the Exmoor Society's archives and there it sat for over forty years, lost, unknown and unread.

Bringing it out into the light has been, for me, one of the things that makes archiving worthwhile. This manuscript is a part of the history of Exmoor and we are fortunate that it sat quietly unnoticed without suffering the fate of many papers and finding its way into landfill. In the forty-five years since it was written, two things have changed its fate. An account of village life in the late 1960s might seem pedestrian in 1970 but in 2015 it is invaluable. And Hope's reputation as a writer and artist has increased so that her work is, rightly, treated more seriously.

Bonham-Carter rejected the manuscript as a piece of local history but in fact that isn't what it is. Hope was not a trained historian and had no pretentions to be one. She was not writing this as a piece of history but as her salute to Withypool. Hope's understanding of the village was enhanced by her understanding of its past. However, she uses vague terms such as "olden times" and she does not distinguish between secondary and primary sources whereas trained historians treat the two differently. For a thoroughly referenced secondary source on Withypool look elsewhere, or turn to the primary sources, the historical record itself rather than the work of historians. Hope won't provide you with academic rigour but she will take you on a tour of Withypool through her eyes, and she was an amazingly shrewd observer. *Exmoor Village* isn't necessarily an accurate account of Withypool's history through the ages, but it is does show one particular woman's view of what village life was like in the 1960s.

A brief note on the text: since Hope had had the opportunity to edit the typescript, I made few changes. Where she referred, for example, to "the last century" this was changed to "the nineteenth century" for the sake of clarity. Place names, which vary in spelling, were standardised using the 1962 Ordnance Survey map, again for clarity. Hope had a tendency to use hyphens to create compound nouns and some of these were removed to make the text easier to read. Choosing the illustrations was something of an adventurous dig through Hope's sketches. It was possible to identify cottages sketched by Hope and it was a lovely coincidence to find one of the cottage described early in the chapter on the walk by Kitridge Lane. Likewise, finding the sketch of one of the last plough teams on Exmoor, celebrated by Hope in the text, was a key moment in helping the text and the illustrations come together. Hope wanted to see this manuscript published and I hope that she would be pleased with the result.

Dr Helen Blackman
Outreach Archivist
The Exmoor Society

[1] Hope Bourne to Victor Bonham-Carter, 1987, Exmoor Society Archives, VBC 13/56.
[2] Victor Bonham-Carter to Hope Bourne, 30/11/1970, Exmoor Society Archives, VBC 13/86.

H. L. B. 1961

CHAPTER ONE

Morning in the Village

Here is Withypool on a bright winter's morning – for this is a book written in winter – with the January sun shining on the river and on the bridge and the road leading down to it, and on the slate roofs still wet with the night's rain. The bare branches of the trees between the river and the moor catch the sunshine in webs of brownish-gold, whilst the long sky-line of the moor itself lies dark above the pale washed green of the little fields that cling to the lower slopes. The cottages that cluster on the hillside that looks to the south turn cheerful faces to the rising sun, for they are most of them white or cream-washed, and only the small low church presents rough grey moorstone to the morning light. There is a good deal of twittering of birds in the cottage gardens, and a few local cars and a Land Rover or two go through, or stop at the Post Office Stores by the bridge, and horsemen clatter by on morning exercise, and dogs bark, and the schoolchildren come out to play, and folk come and go from their front gates, and here again is just another day.

Withypool is not so quiet in the summer, at least not in these times when there are tourists about and many cars on the roads, but just now the village is its own self, and going about its own business as it has done since first it became a place at all. It is a small world on its own, an entity in itself, and its concern is its own parish of wild moorland, scattered farms and patchwork fields. Farming, hunting, gossip, gardening, the weather, the occasional social event – such as a wedding or a funeral – these make the pattern of life here. The radio and the telly, it is true, bring the wider world into almost every home, but here a hold-up in London or war in the Middle East is of far less importance than yesterday's rain or tomorrow's sheep sale.

It is a good time to take another look around the village and make a fresh appraisal of what one has always taken for granted. The hub of the village, the focal point, is the space between the bridge and the Post Office Stores. Here on one side is the Post Office and on the other a small filling station, and here everything with any business in Withypool passes, stops, parks, loads or unloads, and local folk forgather, meet, talk, and gravitate towards the bridge where the low parapets invite one to lean and look at the racing water.

Here below is the river, the Barle, running strong and broad and fast on its way from the moor to its confluence with the Exe away beyond Dulverton, filling the valley always with its singing, and at the moment with a deeper sound, being full after much rain. It is a lovely river, clear and sparkling except in times of spate, and offering much fun to the children of the village, and good fishing also.

The bridge is a fine one, the largest of all the Exmoor bridges. Its six wide arches stride across the river, and its grey stone makes it one with the hills and the boulders of the river bed. But it is not an ancient bridge, being only a brief hundred years old or less. The original bridge of Withypool stood higher up the river, just at the point where there are tall poplar trees. Apparently the old bridge became unsafe, and so an entirely new one was decided upon, and the present one built as it stands today. Local stone and local labour was used, I believe, and so from the first the new bridge was one with the village and its other buildings. On both sides of the river bits of old lane – the original highway of Withypool – still lead to the place where the old bridge stood.

It is pleasant at all times to linger upon the bridge, and lean over the rough-edged parapets and look at the water and at the pleasing views both up and down. Above the bridge the river broadens into a wide pool, very clear and shallow so that one sees the pebbles and boulders of its bed like brown amber, whilst below it falls from the arches over a small ledge, breaking in six spates of white foam into the deeper water. Here in the higher pool the ascending salmon often lie to rest awhile before continuing their journey to the upper reaches, and one may through the clear water see them, like dark submerged submarines, head on to the current, quite motionless except for an occasional flicker of the tail. On a fair winter day it is quite a local occupation to congregate and stand around and 'look for the fish'. The most I ever saw there together were thirteen, salmon I mean. Yes, the bridge is a pleasant place for loitering, and on a summer's evening especially, when the low sun turns the water to a pool of fathomless gold, and the trees bend to their own dark reflections, and time has no more meaning. Then one's thoughts seem loosened, and fly away, and back again. Withypool, Withypool – how did you get your name? Was it from this pool, and the withies on the banks? The erudite may suggest other meanings and another derivation, but I like to think it was so. Long ago the little meads beside the river, now green and enclosed, would have been rush beds overgrown with sallow bushes, and this reach would indeed have been a pool amongst the withies.

Turning again one faces the Post Office. This is our village stores, the Shop. It is the most important establishment in the place, for without it the village as such could hardly exist. Cream washed and neat, it holds within almost everything that can be wanted locally – bread, groceries, household articles, ironmongery, garden tools, Wellington boots, paints and pesticides, stationery, newspapers and magazines, and of course the inevitable stamps and things of the Post Office. In short, one can get anything from a cotton reel to a felling axe. It is a true village shop in the best tradition, serving the needs of a district of scattered hill farms distant from any township. There are always Land Rovers coming and going outside, and horsemen too, for this is hill country and a farming community, and even here in the metropolis one is aware of this. A flock of sheep or a herd of bullocks is often to be encountered here on the road, attended by riders on horseback and the inevitable lean Collie dogs. Not so very long ago the mail went out from here every morning on horseback, for this was a riding round, the last to be so on Exmoor. Now however things have moved on a bit, and modernity caught up with us, and the mail that comes in in the little red van in the dark of the early morning goes out again on its round in a car.

The small filling station that stands opposite, an acknowledgement to modern needs, goes with the stores business. The little edifice that overstands the petrol pumps is a nice little piece of modern work with its raw stone ends and well-pitched roof. (I've always thought I would like it for a summer house if I could pick it up and take it along to my garden). Hereabouts too there are bits of pretty garden, gay with flowers in the summer – and in the spring there are daffodils by the bridge – for our good postmaster is a public-spirited man, and one with a love of gardening, who has done much to make this corner pleasant.

A little way up the road on higher ground is the church. Two dark yew trees guard the gate, which though not old have already the solemn majesty of their kind, and thence steps and a path lead straight up to the church porch. The church itself is a true building of the moor, of weathered grey stone, dark and rough, its general proportions long and low, its tower squat and plain. A simple porch gives access to the door, and the door squeaks and murmurs as one pushes against it to slip inside. The interior is quiet, and light in comparison with many others. A nave, a chancel, the tower at the west end, and an aisle to the north comprise the whole. St Andrew's church – for such it is – is probably of Norman foundation, but the fabric as it stands I would guess to be largely of the fourteenth and fifteenth centuries. The three pointed arches of the aisle argue the former, the windows in general the latter (though I think some of these are modern). The font with its bold, simple ornament, is certainly Norman. The stained glass that fills three of the windows is modern. Everything about the small church – other than the stained glass – is of functional simplicity: the plain timbered roof, the floor of big blue slate flags, the plain-headed windows. Here is no tracery, no carving, no effigies of knights in armour. A moorland parish of long ago had no affluence, no great agricultural wealth, no surplus of riches wherewith to embellish its church with art, no rich merchants to raise a lofty pinnacled tower, no lordly connections to give ornamental tombs. St Andrew's church of Withypool is a simple church of the moor, the offering of a community of hill farmers and a few local landlords.

Stop for a moment, and linger, and face the altar where the sun strikes upon it through the plain latticed window of the chancel side. How many generations have stood here? How many human creatures have come here, in joy, in sorrow, in hope, or fear, in faith and in bitterness, to kneel and pray, some with assurance, some knowing not why, yet all of them reaching out to something that is beyond mortal grasp and understanding? Every stone here is full of the longings of the human heart, and the joy and anguish of life. I feel it here in the silence. Weddings, christenings, funerals, banns and prayers for those in sickness, Sunday service and Communion – all these I have known, and so it has been since the stones were first set. Here is the heart of the little community, to which all come at their beginnings and at their endings.

Outside in the sun again, one may look around at the simple memorials of the families of the parish, and at the tall finger of stone which is the old preaching cross from the plinth of which sermons might be preached in the open air (the upper part of it has been restored). "God's Acre", where it stretches out to the north and east is a pleasant place, and more like a field than most churchyards, with its rough hedge banks and ordinary field gate in the north-east corner. I cross it most days, as it is a short cut between my cottage and my allotment garden. It grows a good crop of hay in the summer, but as nobody seems to want this nowadays, I scrounge most of it for compost. Vegetation usually grows well in a churchyard, I don't know why, though I could make a good guess.

A little further down the road is another place of worship, a small chapel of Wesleyan denomination. It is a neat little place with "gothic" moulding to its door and windows. Just above is the village school, of dark stone, with whitewashed schoolhouse attached. It is still a place of young voices, though the older children now go by bus to Dulverton every day. Retracing one's steps past the church gate one comes to the little nook of lawn and flowers that is Withypool's "public garden". This pretty little patch, entered by a wicket-gate at either end, was laid out as a memorial to one Clair Norton, killed in a car accident, by her sorrowing parents, and given by them to the village. Grass with a seat upon it, flower-beds, flowering cherry trees, azaleas and rhododendrons, a heather bed and a low clipped thorn hedge – it is a pretty nook in which to sit for a few minutes and contemplate the church, the village road, and the moor beyond. The summerhouse of local rough stone, containing another seat, is part of the memorial too, and until recently was the recognised bus shelter for the village (the weekly bus to Minehead drew up just outside, by the churchyard wall), but now we don't have any buses – the transport company are too mean. The larger building, which also occupies a portion of the ground is the Church Room, used for various parish functions. Once, in pre-television days, weekly whist-drives were held here, and they were great fun.

A few paces further on is the Royal Oak Inn, a plain nineteenth-century building set upon the corner, and comprising in itself hotel, bar, and stabling. At the time of writing it is coloured an awful pink – the legacy of some past proprietor who must have liked that colour, though it is hard to understand why – but the new landlord is nobly set on restoring it to its original sober cream.

Across the river, just where "the Hill" begins is the Village Hall, recently rebuilt to modern standards, and pleasantly functional. Most events take place here. This concludes the list of Withypool's public buildings – though perhaps one ought to add the call-box by the Post Office, for it is most useful to folk like me who haven't a 'phone of their own – and shows the extent of our village activities and ambitions.

Of the dwellings, most are cottages, some thirty odd of them, nearly all, upon the north – that is the south-facing side of the valley, though there are a few on the other side of the bridge. The local style is simple: walls of thick rough stone, rendered over and white-or-cream washed on the face , a slate roof of rather shallow pitch, a chimney at either end like two ears, small windows, and a middle front door of "stable" halves. (This last is a most pleasant feature, for to open the top half and let the sunshine into the house, and then to lounge comfortably on the lower half, is one of the minor pleasures of daily life). Such is the traditional pattern, but there are many variations, especially in the more recent dwellings, and in actual fact there are no two houses in the village quite alike – that is, with the exception of the council houses on the far side of the bridge. We have one "contemporary" house. This particular dwelling stands out bravely in the modern idiom upon the northern river slope.

With split-level plan, plate-glass windows and cantilevered balcony, it makes no concession to tradition at all, yet contrives to fit very well into its setting, and is more in harmony with the rhythm of nature than some edifices I could name. Despite my love of the comfort and cosiness and naturalness of the older cottages, I sometimes think it would be great fun to live in a house like this. I feel it would be lovely to sit on that balcony in the evening light, suspended in space, with all that you see flowing to you and under you, as it does when you are on the bridge of a ship. And probably go downstairs to bed – for I think the living room is on the "first floor".

Referring back to the older dwellings, a feature, or rather a method of construction, common to all buildings of the locality from the humblest to the largest is (or was) the setting of any building by means of excavation right into its sloping hillside. This most primitive fashion, followed through the centuries right up to very recent times, and initially coming about from the necessity of contriving a level site from a sloping stony hillside, was adhered to (until the advent of recent queer ideas on the part of the public authorities) because of several natural advantages which such a construction offered in the context of local terrain and climate. Firstly, as said, the delving out of a quarry-like space was the simplest way of making a level floor, secondly the raw stone so broken out could be used straight away for the front and gable ends of the house, thirdly, thus set low with back roof touching the ground the dwelling escaped the wind, and lastly, with face to the sun and back right down in the living hillside, the house was well insulated against all the cold of winter. Such a little home was wonderfully cosy. I know, from first-hand experience. I have lived in a succession of such dwellings in my lifetime, and I know just how warm and comfortable such a home can be in stormy winter weather, and conversely, how cool on hot summer days. Of course the modern fetish is "hygiene" and the dread word "damp". Well again I say I have never found any such dwelling anymore damp than any other in this wild wet country and anyway I have never found that damp in itself ever did anyone any harm. (My present cottage is set well into the hillside, with the living room totally below ground level on two sides, and the last thing I want is to have a senseless "clearance" made around it). The coldest dwellings in Withypool are well-known to be the properly-approved Council houses. Only once has frost ever penetrated my little cottage, and that was in the great winter of '63, when the intense cold just came right in through the front walls.

Beyond the grouping of the village, upon its fringe, there are several "residences", large houses built at varying dates during the present century, more or less as "hunting-boxes" resplendent with stables and staff-quarters. As homes they are substantial and comfortable, but with regard to their architectural merits the less said the better.

The Rectory, that is the present one, is a large bungalow-type dwelling set within a nice piece of timbered ground on the north-east side of the village. Since I have, by the courtesy of the Rector, a good-sized patch of the lower ground for the growing of my vegetables, I will stop here and this may conclude the morning's survey. Such is our village.

CHAPTER TWO

An Evening with Maps and Some Other Things

A soaking wet late afternoon, the rain flying and driving on a rising sou'west gale, stinging one's face with the hardness of hail, penetrating everywhere and making a misery of everything, whilst the wind buffets about, wrenching at one's sou'wester and raincoat, sending the puddles racing, and with sudden gusts swirling the water off the roofs in showers of spray. There is nothing profitable one can do out of doors except get wet – which is not profitable – so the best and most sensible thing to do is to come indoors and make an early evening of it.

Home is a good place at a time like this. Just below, the river is roaring in a yellow-grey spate, foaming along the very tops of its banks, and making uneasy those folk whose houses are on lower ground (for we have had thirteen days of unceasing rain, and the river can be expected to flood at any moment if the downpour does not ease), but my little cottage is on rising ground, so I have no need to worry. The voice of the river follows me indoors, and then I light the lamp and draw the curtains and shut it out. Tonight is a good night to study maps and documents and to do "paper work" for which daylight and sunshine are too precious, and to travel in imagination in time as well as space.

Maps are the best of all literature and I love them. I have about a score here to hand, all relating to Exmoor in general and Withypool in particular, beginning with the First Ordnance Survey of 1809 and ending with the latest published Tourist Map. A map is visual history, and tells one so much more than mere words, and adventure also, for as I've said it takes one travelling far and wide in comfort on a night like this. And ancient documents too, dull as they may seem at first sight, are full of interest when one relates them to the place and life around one. So I have quite a pile of transcripts about me now, and they pay for delving into between tea and supper.

Maps, deeds, and records – what has history to say of Withypool under the moor? Not a great deal in words, and one must guess the greater part "reading between the lines", supplementing written history with the evidence of things around, and judging from what one knows oneself about the country and its yesterdays in general. The oldest documentary reference to Withypool is a brief entry in the Domesday Book of 1086. Then, as from the thirteenth century onwards there are various documents relating to the Forest of Exmoor, most of which in one way or another have some passing references to Withypool. Then come the Parish Registers which begin in 1653. Then the first mile-to-the-inch Ordnance Map which followed the survey of Devon and Somerset in the early 1800s, and which shows Withypool in the context of the countryside of the time. From round about the end of the eighteenth century there is Parson Boyce's Hunting Diary, which, though it does not relate specifically to Withypool, has frequent references to the district, and is relevant in as much as Parson Boyce was sometime Rector of Withypool and lived in the village. There also exist manorial records for the Manor of Landacre, but I have not had access to these. There are two lists of the free suitors. The great Tithe Map of the parish (which I had the pleasure of browsing over only yesterday, by kindness of the Rector) dates from about 1839 – the exact date on the parchment is smudged – and presents the local topography in greatest detail. Lastly, there is the present Ordnance Survey series, begun I think in 1870, consisting of various one-inch, two and a half-inch, and six-inch sheets.[1]

Unfortunately all the records and papers of the Acland estate, which were lodged at Exeter, went up in flames in the "blitz" on that city in the last war, and so Withypool has lost a good deal of probably interesting historical material, for the Aclands were, I believe, extensive landowners in the district, as well as Wardens of the Forest.

[1] The 6" to 1 mile scale for mountain and moorland was agreed from 1863.

Looking back to the beginning, travelling in time as far as one may, one sees first the moor, the great waste, the primaeval wilderness, as it was before man's hand was laid upon it, its hilltops flayed by the wind even as today, its valleys choked with scrub, and its big river running from its source in the heights onwards through marsh and sallow-thickets to meet the wet enveloping forest which darkened all the lower land. Then the first footsteps, of hunters of the game upon the hills, men of the Stone Age who have left us no trace, and those of the Bronze Age who gave us the lonely round barrows on the hilltops. Then the settlers, Celtic or Saxon, those very first pioneers who carved little farmsteads from the waste and made their homes in the wild land. Then a little settlement, a group of dwellings, a place of gossip and exchange, taking root by the ford of the river just where it emerges from the wilder hills into a shallower, sunnier place. A church, a mill, then a bridge – the picture grows.

The eleventh century, when our history proper begins, finds all the wild hill country to the north west of Withypool apparently already held by the Crown as Royal Forest, a hunting ground reserved for the sport of princes, and probably Withypool itself included therein, though this is by inference only.

The Domesday entry says: "Robert (de Olburville) holds half a hide in Widepolle. Three foresters, Dodo, Almer held it in parage… There is land for four ploughs. From this land Robert used to pay 20 shillings to the King's ferm at Winesford (Winsford). Now it has been declared to be theign-land".

One has to make one's own deductions from this rather laconic entry. Robert held land in Withypool, not a vill[2] or manor in its entirety, as did all his fellow land holders round about. It is rather difficult to understand what the circumstances were. There is no mention of other holders, nor of villeins or stock, or land other than that for the four ploughs, such as feature in most other entries. For the holding of his half-hide it seems Robert had to pay something to the King's personal estate of Winsford. The declaration that the land was "theign-land" meant that the holder thereof had, when called upon, to do service to the king on horseback. That Robert's predecessors were specified as "foresters" is significant, both as indicating the existence of the Forest as such at that time, and in implying a close connection between Withypool and the said Forest from the earliest times.

One is left with the conclusion that Withypool was from the beginning attached in some way to the Royal Forest, and at the time of the Domesday survey was not considered to be taxable as a whole as were

[2] A vill was the smallest administrative unit under the feudal system.

the other vills. This theory is strengthened by the peculiar institution of the free suitors, whereby the farmers of Withypool and the sister parish of Hawkridge, but of no other Exmoor parish, had certain complex rights and duties within the Forest as from "time out of mind" until the final disafforestation.

One wonders how it all began – which came first, the Forest as such or the established parish and village? Did the bounds of the Forest encroach on the lands of the early settlement and the men of Withypool bargain for their rights with promise of service? Or did the little village amongst the withy-beds grow up under the royal patronage of the West Saxon kings, allowed to take root upon the ground mid-way between the royal manor and the royal hunting ground on conditions of service given when called upon? We shall never know, but Withypool has ever been more closely associated with the Royal Forest than any other parish, and was, and is, most truly a village of the moor.

Later history certainly finds Withypool within the confines of the Forest, together with some ten other Somerset parishes – all unlawfully afforested by King John. John was an insatiable hunter and a great land-grabber, and did not hesitate to lay hands on all the best deer coverts and incorporate them in his hunting grounds. He even went so far as to declare the whole of Devon to be Forest, and though he stopped short of treating all Somerset likewise he did, it seems, put the lands of those manors or parishes as far east as Porlock Vale within the bounds of his Forest of Exmoor. Under the terms of the Magna Carta, however, he was forced to promise the disafforestation of all such lands. The subsequent Carta de Foresta (1217) furthered these promises of the Crown, but government machinery being at all times slow, it was a long time before anything definite was done about it.

In 1278 the first recorded "perambulation" of Exmoor Forest took place, its purpose being to define the proper and lawful bounds of same.[3] This first circuit, beginning at County Gate, put the bounds on this side of the moor as running along the River Exe to Road Castle (an earth work to the north-west of Room Hill), thence to Hernsbarrow (an ancient barrow on Room Hill), and then on by the Wambarrows (on the summit of Winsford Hill) to Ashway and the Dane's Brook. By this both Withypool and Hawkridge were left wholly within the Forest. However, later in the same year a second perambulation took place, starting from Willingford – possibly the inhabitants of Withypool and Hawkridge had protested – and by this the bounds were set to run from "Wyveleford"

[3] E.T. MacDermot in *A History of the Forest of Exmoor* (1973, p. 17) states that perambulations were made in 1219, 1279, 1298 and 1300 but only of the Somerset boundary, not the Devon boundary.

(Willingford) in a straight line to "Shyreburnesse" (Sherdon Hutch) and down the river to "Langaker" (Landacre) "leaving that within the Forest", then to "Stonhuste" (a stone that must have existed somewhere at the head of the little combe that has always marked the boundary of Landacre on the east), then to "Dermark" (possibly the small barrow with the white stone in the middle of Bradymoor), thence to "She...combesheved" (Shutcombe Head), and so on by the present Exford-Simonsbath boundary. By this all of Hawkridge and Withypool, with the exception of Landacre, was put out of the Forest. A further perambulation took place in 1298, which in general confirmed the bounds as set by the preceding one, but with some uncertainty as to Landacre. An appended list of all the local lands and manors now disafforested and outside the bounds, includes Landacre. But the actual bounds at this point are still "Deresmark" and "Stonehiste", and one can only suppose that the boundary now ran across Bradymoor in a line to – or from – Sherdon Hutch. Unless, in the first place, "Stonehuste" or "Stonehiste" were not the head of the Landacre comb, but some place further west, and the "Dermark" likewise so. In this case though the original inclusion of Landacre is difficult. By the Forest survey of 1651 the boundary between the said Forest and the lands of Withypool was noted to follow the line which is still that dividing the present-day parishes of Simonsbath and Withypool.

The people of Withypool and other neighbouring parishes must have been glad indeed to be free of the Forest and Forest Law. Within the Forest a code of law prevailed, based on the absolute preservation of game, which was harsh and restrictive far beyond the common law of England. The further enclosing of land was strictly forbidden, as was any activity which might be detrimental to wildlife, and for the killing of deer a man might be hanged, blinded, or otherwise mutilated. It is true that after 1217 the latter savage punishments were commuted to fines, but fines that were very heavy and severe to a countryman.

Nevertheless, the Forest and its matters were always very close to Withypool, and Withypool bound closely to the Forest in many ways, and its story one and the same. The affairs of the Forest were administered by various officials, the warden, foresters, verderers, regarders etc., and of these foresters, holding something of the position of modern gamekeepers, were as much hated by the country folk as ever their nineteenth-century equivalents were. Offences against Forest Law were tried by special courts presided over by appointed Justices-in-Eyre, and it is from the still-existing rolls of these courts or Forest Eyres that so much of our own local history can be gleaned. Matters appertaining to the depasturing that was allowed were attended to by the Swainmote courts (of which more later).

Men poached, as they have always done, or committed other offences against the Forest, and their names and addresses got put down on the parchment of the Court rolls together with the nature of their offences and consequent fines. The several rolls of the Forest Eyres and Inquisitions which still exist, dating collectively from 1257 to 1376, are full of items of interest, vignettes of life such as Adam of Newland, Hamlin of Blackland and some others of Withypool heaving out peat without warrant, or Hugh of Landacre having unfairly taken in a patch of ground. More interesting though than the exact nature of the offences is the fact that the coupling of a man's name with the name of a place definitely establishes that this or that farm or settlement was in existence at the given date. Of course in this context the fact that some farms never find mention at all does not mean that they did not exist, but merely that the occupant was a law-abiding citizen or – more likely – did not get himself caught, and so drew no attention to his homestead.

Until the establishment of Simonsbath house and farm in 1654, the acting forester seems to have abode in Withypool, probably at Landacre, (there were at one time two farms and a couple of cottages there) for it was at Landacre that the Swainmote Courts were held, and it was right on the edge of the Forest. In Withypool itself was the Pound wherein estrays found in the Forest were penned until otherwise disposed of. (The site of the Pound was the corner of land between the butt of the old bridge and that of the new on the south side of the river). It was from Withypool that the free suitors set off to "drive the Forest" when called upon.

So before Simonsbath existed all the business connected with the Forest was more or less transacted from Withypool, and in this way the village would have had some importance. The added aisle of the church would seem to indicate some expansion in the later Middle Ages. The enlarging of what has always been technically – so the Rector tells me – a chapel-of-ease to Hawkridge is significant. Afterwards though, when affairs shifted to Simonsbath, Withypool may be assumed to have slipped back into being just another little hill-country village.

Documents of the sixteenth and seventeenth centuries referring to matters of the moor give glimpses of a local life concerned with much the same things as before and since – sheep and cattle, the straying thereof, common rights, tithes, boundary disputes, and of course poaching.

The Parish registers, beginning in the seventeenth century, are for the first few pages practically illegible, but thereafter give a fair record of families moving from one farm to another as sons grew up, married, and took on tenancies that became vacant. One item of passing interest is the fairly frequent number of baptisms where the mother is described as "unmarried". If society was not then "permissive", at least some folk did without permission.

The first issue of the Ordnance Map for West Somerset, printed in 1809, shows Withypool set in the midst of a countryside of wild unenclosed moorland. To the north and west lies Withypool Common, Exmoor Forest and its other attendant commons, sweeping in one vast stretch from Porlock to Bratton Fleming, to the east Exford South Common and Roony Hill lap against the bounds, to the south east is Winsford Hill, while to the south lie the Hawkridge moors. A wild landscape it must have been, but one to have delighted and exhilarated the horseman and hunter, when like Parson Boyce he might have ridden after the great hounds of Sir Thomas Acland as they pursued the flying stag across the unfenced bent and heather.

As to those days of hard riding, Parson Boyce's hunting diary remains as a stimulating memorial. It is at present in the possession of Colonel Gilbert Collyns of Dulverton, and I had the pleasure of seeing it once.[4] Its large size, its fine faded writing, its odd sketches of stags' antlers, arouse a longing to browse over it, and live with some of those great runs, and see the countryside as it was, unspoilt with poles and wires, unencumbered with motor traffic, and unthreatened by reservoirs and holiday camps. Parson Boyce was one of those eighteenth century "sporting" clergymen with which the West Country abounded, men brought up to the life of the land, who rode and hunted and shot and farmed their own glebe as well as any, and probably understood their parishioners the better for it. (Some, it is true, neglected their religious duties for these pursuits, but in the main they were good men with their feet on the ground as well as their heads in the clouds). He reigned at Withypool and Hawkridge from sometime in the latter part of the 18th century to 1834 first as curate and then as Rector, and as the living was then – or so I am told – a very good one compared with most moorland parishes, he could probably afford good horses. I like to think of him sitting by the fire of the house still remembered as his – it is the one next door to me as I write, on the west side – perhaps on such a night as this, stretched out to the blaze after a hard day in the saddle in the teeth of rough weather, and anon reaching for his pen and book to add his most recent recollections of yet another day's sport.

With the early years of the nineteenth century came the disafforestation and sale for enclosure of Exmoor Forest, and its following repercussions on the pattern of Withypool life, especially in the matter of grazing rights. But more of this later.

As to the internal matters of the parish, the Tithe Map of 1839 is a great

[4] Colonel Gilbert Collyns's (d. 1974) papers are now in the possession of the Somerset Heritage Centre.

document – literally, in matter of size, for it is so large one can only spread it out on a cleared floor space. Herein one may see, looking down with almost aerial view, the district exactly as it was 130-odd years ago, with every house, every building, every hedge marked, and every parcel of ground, from the largest field to the smallest plot, recorded and numbered. (Unfortunately the record book which should accompany the map, giving field names and ownership, seems to be lost). Dwelling houses are marked in red, other buildings in black. Here one can see and note what changes have taken place since then, what houses have been built since, what fallen into decay. In the general pattern of land, the change has been very little, but one does notice that here and there small fields have since been amalgamated into larger ones, the banks having either fallen down or been cast down. But the tendency to larger fields is one that continues everywhere nowadays.

But one comes out of the past of documents and written things into that of human memory – of living memory and the remembrances of parents and grandparents. So I think another chapter is indicated.

CHAPTER THREE

Memories of Yesterday

My own memories of Withypool and district go back twenty years, and in that time I have had the good fortune to know various good folk whose memories are longer than that, and who themselves remember the tales and anecdotes their parents and grandparents told them. Thus first-hand recollection goes back quite a way.

There are, or used to be, echoes of the old packhorse days. Once all Exmoor was packhorse country, for there were no roads over the moor fit to carry wheeled vehicles, and everything had to come and go by hack-pony. All commodities, all farm produce, all merchandise, went by crook and pannier, and travellers rode on horseback. This hill country of the West was the last to know the trotting of the packhorse, or to see the corn come in upon the backs of plodding ponies.

Carts became general in the region only after the Knight family, following their purchase of Exmoor in 1818, had set an example of good road making over the high moor and had themselves brought in waggons and teams. According to tradition, the first cart to come into Withypool did so one Sunday morning in 1830. Folk were in church when it arrived, and all came out to see this marvel on wheels. It seems it had been purchased by the then owner of Weatherslade farm, a certain Mr Quartley, a man with progressive ideas, and had been brought all the way from a township on the eastern side of the moor – Carhampton, I think – travelling with great difficulty no doubt over the rough tracks and through the narrow tunnel-like lanes of the hill country. Tradition does not record just what sort of a cart it was, but most probably it was of the pattern known as a "railcart", the kind most generally in use upon the farms round about here until recently.

Once an elderly lady residing in the district told me that when as a child she and her family used to spend their holidays in Withypool, they stayed upon a farm – South Hill I think she said it was – and that she could remember seeing in one of the tallets a whole pile of old packhorse gear lying in disuse. This would be about eighty years ago, I should guess. I wonder what happened to it? I expect it got burnt when someone got around to tidying up the tallet one day.

The house known as "Greystones" is still remembered as Parson Boyce's, though of the old sporting parson himself little is recollected. The official Rectory house – for the joint parishes of Withypool and Hawkridge – was for long the large dwelling down by the river at Tarr Steps, now the Tarr Steps Hotel. A strange place for a Rectory one would think, at the foot of the woods and miles from anywhere, shut in by the hills and the river. However, the name "Parsonage" attached to the farm above would seem to indicate that this was once glebe land, and so hence the probable reason for the siting. The present Rectory here in Withypool was built in the 1920s and is a more convenient residence for the incumbent, that is so far as Withypool is concerned, though often entailing difficult journeying to Hawkridge in winter weather.

As to local goings-on, there exists a nasty little rhyme which says: "steal a sheep and sell the wool and ring the bells of Withypool". Just what that may imply is best left to the imagination, I think!

During the past century, and up to the earlier years of the present one, Withypool village was, if not a place of any great importance in the wider context of the country, at least a very busy one within itself. It was, like all of its kind in the days before easy motor transport, self-contained and self-supporting. It had, so I am told, a bakery, a grocery store, a smithy, a wheelwright's yard (established after carts became general in the district), a carpenter's shop, and a bootmender's, and also a tailor's business and of course its own corn mill. Altogether it catered for its community of hill farmers very well and adequately.

For wants beyond these there were the townships of Dulverton and North Molton, both about nine miles distant on the edge of the moor, and farther afield the market towns of South Molton and Bampton, and the borough of Barnstaple. A carrier's cart used to plod slowly but surely between Withypool and North Molton for the benefit of those who had not transport of their own, and another one plied from Dunster. The fare I believe was sixpence.

The coming of the Taunton to Barnstaple Railway in 1873, with its station and goods yard at Dulverton, opened the way to the wider world, or at least made access easier. (Its recent closure is much to be regretted).

The pattern of farming was fundamentally one of stock raising, but nevertheless a considerable amount of corn was grown in the district. There was enough for local needs and to spare. Oats for stock feed, wheat for bread corn, and some barley as well. The land hereabouts will grow good corn. (I myself have seen black oats grown at 1200 feet come up in sheaves as big and heavy as midland ones, and have helped to stook good wheat at 1100 feet). The difficulty is in harvesting, for not only is the climate here a wet one generally, but it seems to rain most frequently in the harvest months. The only thing that will get corn good under such conditions is hand labour, and that I think was the secret of success in the old days. The constant turning of sheaves and the making of "windmows" were the means whereby the corn was saved in the face of inclement weather. Once the lines of beehive-shaped windmows marching across the stubble fields were a feature of the autumn landscape, but nowadays there is only one farm in the parish which still grows corn – an average of five acres of oats each year.

As to the beasts of the farms, they were the traditional red Devon cattle and the native Exmoor sheep. It is not far from here to Molland, the home of the best strains of Devon cattle, as bred by the Quartleys. The Closewool too, after its evolution as a breed, became a sheep of the locality.

The village on the whole seems to have had more dwellings a hundred years ago than today. A comparison with the Tithe Map shows that a number which then existed have now quite gone or have been demoted into sheds and outbuildings. However, some have been built since, so perhaps the balance is fair enough. All the old dwellings of the village were small cottages, and when the first substantial house was built (In 1860 I think – the date stone is somewhat weathered) that to the west of the church, it was thought so grand that it received the name of "the Palace" from Withypool folk, and is still known as such locally.

The Royal Oak inn as it stands today is fairly modern. The original inn was what is now known as Oak Cottage, set back behind the present edifice, and surrounded by stables. This small place used to have a wide wooden balcony at the east end, whereon folk might sit to drink their liquor pleasantly in the open air, but this has now gone. The site of the existing inn-hotel used to be just a triangle of grass with, traditionally, a large oak tree upon it. When workmen were making some alterations at the back of the premises a few years ago they unearthed the root-stock of a big ancient oak just there—perhaps the original tree from which the inn took its name.

The church was restored in the Victorian era, happily without doing much damage to its character.[5] In 1881[6] the chapel of Wesleyan denomination was built. This building, already referred to, is a nice little bit of architecture, with ogee drip-stones over the windows and door. The present Council school was built in 1877 and opened the following year with an attendance of eighty pupils. The schoolmaster's salary was fixed at £1 a week. Prior to this there was a tiny private school in the village, held in one room of a local storekeeper's house, and for the privilege of attending this the children paid, I believe, the sum of twopence a week.[7]

The primary fuel of the village was peat, supplemented by brushwood from the hedges. Thus peat cutting was an important summer occupation upon the Hill. All sorts of odd tales I have heard of this, such as folk getting lost for a while upon the common when the hill mist clapped in suddenly. The old cuttings or hags can still be seen – or fallen over into – in various place on the Hill. No-one, however, cuts peat today. The last farm in the parish to do so was Knighton. Friends who lived there often told me of the summer evenings spent turf cutting up above the farm. The clats[8] were prized out with a long spade-like tool and set up on end to dry. Afterwards they were carted down to the farm and built into ricks or "turf burrows". Local peat it seems came in two sorts: spine turf and pit turf. The former consisted of clats skimmed from the surface and of a light rooty nature, and the latter of stuff dug from a bog pit, dense and black. The latter was considered the best. When dry it was as good as coal. I have occasionally got myself a bit of such peat, and it makes a lovely fire, especially when mixed with hedge beech wood. The scent of it is exquisite. The old hearth fires never went out, or hardly so, for the embers would smoulder all night, waiting to be blown into life in the morning. The ash from such fires has always been known and valued as a spring dressing, so the peat firing had a double value, first as a fuel and then as a fertilizer.

The common-rights, as may be readily understood, meant a great deal to the folk of Withypool, and until 1921 all such matters were dealt with by the Manorial Court Leet, which assembled about once in three years. This Court, at which payable dues were settled and fines for misdemeanours – offences against the accepted rules of common grazing etc. –

---

[5] It was restored in 1887 and then again in 1902, when the tower was also rebuilt. (Exmoor National Park Historic Environment Record, ENPHER).

[6] Hope was unsure of the date and the typescript just has "18" and then a gap for the last two digits. This date is taken from (ENPHER).

[7] The school was closed in 1970.

[8] John Downes *Dictionary of Devon Dialect* gives "clat" as an alternative to "clod". Collins Dictionary also states that it can mean "an irksome or troublesome task".

imposed, met either at the residence of the Lord of the Manor (which during most of the nineteenth century was Newland), or at the Royal Oak inn. Such an occasion was in true Exmoor fashion, an excuse for a good feast. A bill of 1821 lists items for a hefty dinner of beef, vegetables and bread, plus grog. Exmoor appetites have always matched its vigorous life! The Law of Property Act of 1922, which put an end to Copyhold, finally brought these Courts and customs to a finish in that year.

One of the chief requirements for the maintenance and improvement of grassland in this country of predominantly acid soil was, and is, lime. The nearest source in former times was Newland in Exford (not to be confused with Newland in Withypool) where there was an outcrop of limestone rock. Here a quarry pit was dug for the extraction of this rare and invaluable substance, and a lime kiln built. Fuel for the burning however, in the form of culm or soft coal, had to be brought all the way from Porlock Weir, whence it came by ship across the Channel from Wales. It was the local custom for farmers to fetch their own coal from the weir for their quota of lime, and often I have heard from a particular farmer friend of the arduousness of such an undertaking. Of how as a boy he had to arise at three o'clock in the morning and take the waggon and horse all the way to Porlock Weir, and back with the coal to the Newland kiln, a total journey of about thirty miles, with steep hills to struggle up all the way, and equally steep gradients to slither down. Coal and limestone were then packed in layers in the kiln and fired, and then after the burning and cooling the rich residue had to be hauled to the farm and spread. So much time and labour! Now the lime-spreading contractors just come in with their lorries, sacks and spinner, and the whole job is done in an hour or so.

John Page passed this way whilst engaged in his "Exploration of Exmoor" and in his subsequent book of that title he remarked of Withypool that "there is nothing particularly interesting about the village, it is true but the scenery is pleasant, and the wild downs across the river form a fine contrast to the luscious-looking water meadows below the white cottages...".[9] He also noted that the church tower was in a ruinous state, the roads rough, but the fishing excellent. The most notable inhabitant of the time seems to have been a certain "foolish woman", but in just what way she was "foolish", whether in mind, ways or witchcraft, he does not say. Upon encountering her, he simply beat a hasty retreat without entering into conversation.

At some time in the later nineteenth, or the earlier years of the twentieth century, Withypool became "known" to outside folk. Despite

[9] Page's book was first published in 1890.

Page's not very favourable comments, tourists and hunting people began to find its virtues of unspoilt countryside and pleasant living much to their liking, and to come to the district. The "Royal Oak" developed as a sporting hotel, with fishing and stabling attached. One by one a number of "residences" were built and cottages converted for the habitation of those who, having first come as visitors, desired to stay as residents. Withypool being in the heart of the hunting country, most of the new folk came to hunt and ride, and stables were erected beside or behind most of the dwellings (Withypool is still full of stabling).

Writers and artists also seem to have felt the attractiveness of Withypool. R.D. Blackmore stayed for a while at the Royal Oak, during the time that he was writing "Lorna Doone", and it is said that he walked a lot in Pennycombe and drew inspiration for much of his scenery description from the rocky upper reaches of this picturesque valley. Walter Raymond came to reside at the quaint little cottage which bears his plaque and his name, and which is now so sadly derelict. In more recent times Sir Alfred Munnings lived for some years in the village, at the house called "the Palace", and is still much talked of.

Horsemen's country this has always been, and still is, and until recently the postal round was a riding one. Horseback was, after all, the simplest way of getting round the parish, from farm to farm, before the days of tarmac. The last of the riding postmen was John Blackmore who then lived and farmed at Waterhouse. Each morning at seven o'clock he used to set out upon his horse "Shamrock" on his fifteen-mile round. His way lay across moor and fields, through fords and along deep muddy lanes and often in the worst possible weather. The clop of hooves in the various farmyards announced the arrival of the Royal Mail. Seldom can letters have had so adventurous a circuit! It is said that on hunting days the mail was sometimes unaccountably late!

Our late Rector, the Reverend Phillip Hopkinson, also rode his parish rounds on horseback. I remember him well, mounted on his nice chestnut gelding, Limerick. In this he shared with the Reverend Brunskill of Oare the distinction of being the last riding parson on Exmoor.

Motor cars, I suppose, began to make a general appearance about the 1920s. When the bus services started I don't know, but alas, they ended about two years ago. Up till then we had a Saturday bus to Minehead and a Friday one to Barnstaple (from Chibbet Post at the top of Halsgrove Lane), but now we have neither, and travel beyond walking distance is difficult for persons not possessing a car.

In pre-television days pleasures and amusements had to be largely home-made. In the summer various sports and gymkhanas and the Flower Show got organized, and in the winter there was a round of whist-drives, dances and parties. Withypool pony races were for long big local events. The race-course was upon the flattish top of Bradley Ham, and the races themselves were for ponies classed by height. I remember the occasions, the big crowds of local folk, and the hearty excitement. It was all great fun, and I don't know why it came to an end, which it did about fifteen years ago. As for the winter entertainments, they went on from November to Lent, with weekly whist-drives in the Church Room, and frequent bigger ones in the Hall. The great "Poultry Whist Drive" held the week before Christmas, all the prizes being poultry and the Champion prize being the biggest possible goose, was the highlight of the season. Christmas farmhouse parties were wonderful affairs, with guests arriving on horseback, feasts spread on long tables, and whist played until midnight. (Whist has always been a favourite game with Exmoor folk). Then of course there was the Harvest supper and St Andrew's Feast, with more eating and whist. How well I remember it all! Happy days!

Of the war years many tales are told. The local Home Guard was formed, as was proper to this region, as a mounted body. The element of sport seems to have entered into most of its exercises and general doings, and a good time to have been had by all. The ammunition issued came in very useful at a time when rabbits were plentiful and the meat ration short. As to the matter of rationing in general, I am assured that it barely existed at all in these parts. Exmoor folk have never cared a hoot about bureaucracy, and such commodities as butter, cream and eggs were always forthcoming in Withypool.

The last momentous happening of recent years was the great flood of 1952. On that fearful August night of the great cloudburst on the Forest the Barle came down in a tremendous torrent sweeping all before it, carrying away everything in its path. On the whole though, the damage was less in Withypool than at places both higher up or lower down the valley. Most of the dwellings of the village are set fairly high above flood level, and the total of houses washed out was I think about ten. Mercifully there was no loss of life. Both Withypool and Landacre bridges stood up to the raging waters, which says much for the construction of both the new and the old. The trail of wreckage all down the valley though was dreadful, with the carcasses of sheep and even cattle tossed up into the trees, and all the fords, stepping-stones and minor bridges washed away. It was many years before the scars of that grim night were erased by nature and the hand of man.

Of tragedies such as come to human lives in most places sooner or later, the most sorrowfully remembered is that of the Sunday School outing of 1952 when a bus load of young folk went with their Rector, Michael Etherington, to Instow sands for the day. At the very end of what had been a most enjoyable occasion, one of the boys went out into the running tide and was caught in a welter of quicksands and cross currents. He cried for help, and the Rector went to his aid, and both were overwhelmed and drowned. This most unhappy thing cast a shadow over Withypool for a long while, and is still not forgotten.

Since then nothing of very great note has occurred in the parish. Life goes on day by day. Folk live, and sometimes die, and the years are punctuated by marriages, births and deaths. Property changes hands, and new folk come to the district from time to time. A few minor alterations occur. But Withypool is still itself.

Speaking of funerals, the most moving that I ever remember was that of May Common of Higher Blackland, in 1960, her two dogs being the chief mourners. Miss May Common had lived and farmed at Blackland with her two sisters for many years, and had been accustomed to "look" the sheep on the higher fields each evening, the three dogs going with her. Then one spring evening she did not return, nor did the dogs. Now this latter was unusual, for if May in the course of her walk met one of the neighbouring farmers and stopped for a lengthy gossip (all Exmoor folk love a gossip), the dogs would get fed up and come home. Eventually, becoming worried, one of her sisters went to look for her. She found her lying under a hedge upon the Top Allotments, having died from a sudden heart attack, with the three dogs close beside her. They had not left her, nor would they leave her then. Not until her body was brought home in a Land Rover would they come home too.

We took the dogs to the funeral. They followed the coffin into the church and up the aisle to the chancel steps and then sat with May's sisters in the front pew, just as though they understood everything. Then they followed the coffin again to the graveside. There were not many dry eyes in the large congregation, I think, for even amongst the men there was a good deal of blowing of noses. Goldy, Roger and Bob, two spaniels and a collie cross, they too are part of the story of Withypool.

CHAPTER FOUR

The Hill

Brooding over the village, dominating it at all seasons, is the Hill, Withypool Common. This wide tract of open moorland, accounting for half the acreage of the parish – 1866 acres to be precise – constitutes one of the very few true remaining commons of Exmoor, and has from "time out of mind" been as it is today, a wild waste and a grazing ground, forming one of the cornerstones of the pastoral economy of the parish.

Withypool Hill! I look up to it every morning and every evening, both from my front gate and my back garden, and see it in all weathers and know it in all its moods. I see it streaked with snow, black and sodden with winter rain, tawny-gold with the bleaching winds of spring, and heather-crowned with the purple glory of high summer. Sometimes it is cloaked in grey mist, sometimes the high clouds race over it in a wild blue sky and its skyline calls to me to be up and away, and sometimes the winds blow so cold over its brow that one's breath chokes at facing them. It is the primaeval land, as it was in the beginning, and the green fields below are cosy and homely when one comes down to them again.

Its heathy wastes begin only a stone's throw away, right by the top houses of the village, and one's feet may be upon it in the space of a few minutes. There are few days when I do not go out to the common. In its broad extent of nearly 2000 acres, one may find every aspect of West Country moorland, every sort of vegetation, every type of height or hollow, and there are places to suit every mood and nooks to catch the sun or evade the wind at all times of the day. One might make a study of native Exmoor right here within this one tract. Perhaps I will try.

Topographically, the main mass of the common consists of twin hills, Withypool Hill proper and Brightworthy Hill, respectively 1306 and 1398 feet high, from which watershed drop four main combes, to wit Knighton Combe on the north, Westwater to the east, Dillacombe to the north-west, and the Halscombe or Willingford water to the south. (Westwater would seem to owe its contradictory name to its flowing from the west). Beyond the river however, to the north-west, there lies another portion, having something of a separate character, which is known as Bradymoor.

The underlying geology is of Devonian sandstones and shales, and the surface soil black peat, and between the two is shillit and usually a "pan" of a skimming of clay. Heather clothes much of the common, capping Withypool Hill itself, sweeping down the long slopes to Knighton Combe and out to the Porchester's Post area, and lapping the south-west side of Brightworthy Hill. Bradymoor is predominantly heather-moor. The heather is principally *Calluna vulgaris*, the common heather, with, wherever there are sunny bits of bank, an intermingling of *Erica cinerea*, the gloriously royal purple bell-heather. Where the ground is damper the shell-pink headed *Erica tetralix* grows. Sometimes, wandering over the heathery stretches, one may come across rarer sorts, white varieties of any of the three species, or rarer still, the carmine-red strain of bell-heather – but in truth, I think there is nothing lovelier than just the amethyst heads of the common heather. (So often we tend to value a thing simply because it is rare and not because it is the most beautiful of its kind).

On high ground there is bog. The most notable patches are those upon Brightworthy Hill, that below Four Fields, and the two upon Bradymoor. There are as well some stretches which qualify as "wet ground", if not as bog proper . Here are to be found all the plants for whom such conditions provide a suitable home. Rushes of at least two species, the cotton-grass which in June lifts its tufty white heads like big snowflakes above the bog, sedges of various sorts, the sphagnum moss that mats itself all around wherever there is moisture enough, and many delicate flowers in season – bog-asphodel, bog-bean, marsh-violet, bog-pimpernel, marsh St John's wort, sundew, the fragile ivy-leaved bell flower and others. An expedition to the bog-ground in early summer when the dragonflies flirt above the pools and the wet warmth comes up like a breath to one's face is like a jungle exploration in miniature. I hardly need say though that one needs caution in so venturing, for the bog-ground is very treacherous, with sticky oozing sucking liquid black peat waiting for the unwary foot that slips between the tussocks and the hags. Just how dangerous any one of these bogs may be, I am not prepared to say, but I give them the benefit of the doubt in as much as I treat them with great respect. Sheep are not infrequently trapped to their death in them, and I know of at least two instances of cows being engulfed.

Some areas of grass moor intermingle with the heather stretches. Bent fescue, nardus and molinia are the common grasses, the latter predominating where the ground is dampish. Brightworthy Hill, on its summit and northern side, is mainly a mixture of grass and bog, and in this is different from Withypool Hill (which as aforementioned is by nature all heather). Some underlying geological difference must make the distinction.

Fern or bracken cloaks most of the steep combe sides, and intermingles with the other vegetation where it can, especially on the northern side of the common and on the Bradymoor part.

Whortleberry spreads in places, and makes some thick stands, especially on banks. Its pink bells are lovely in spring, and its dark blue berries delicious in summer.

Gorse – or furze as it is more commonly known – is prevalent in places and is of two species, the common gorse and the dwarf or western gorse. The former flowers in spring, and if one lets it, will grow into a gnarled shrub of seven or more feet high (though it seldom does, since it mostly gets burnt before it attains this size). The dwarf gorse, as its name implies, is small and low-growing, seldom reaching a height of more than a foot, and flowers in the autumn when its golden blossoming intermingling with the heather makes a wonderful tapestry of colour across the moor. When left to itself though it does make a thick spiny mat which is more or less impenetrable.

Of wild life, foxes and hares are the common ground creatures of the Hill, though rabbits are beginning to appear here and there once again (being by now fairly recovered from the myxomatosis of some fifteen years ago).[10] A hare of the Hill is nearly as fine a sight as a fox, being as equally red in the summer, and big and strong too. Once there were polecats in these parts. One assumes them to have become extinct, but one can never be quite sure. Not very many years ago one of the men of Withypool killed a "fitchee" on the hill which was said to be a true wild polecat by those who subsequently saw it. Unfortunately, it is not always easy, except for the expert naturalist, to tell the difference between a true native polecat and a ferret gone wild. (There used to be many ferrets kept by local folk in the old rabbiting days). Yet I have a feeling that more wild creatures of a rarer sort still exist in the remote and wild places of our land than we generally credit. If they keep well out of man's way, man is

[10] Myxomatosis first appeared in Britain in 1953.

not likely to see them except for an occasional and uncertain glimpse.

Moorland birds of all sorts are to be seen on or above the Hill. The handsome native black grouse are beginning to increase again (they were almost exterminated by the great winter of 1963), and one may once more put up a fine black cock as one goes striding through the heather. The curlew calls above in the days of spring, its lovely cry coming down the wind like the very spirit of the moor set loose. The lapwings and the golden plover come also in due season, and larks abound. Chats, wheatears and all manner of small birds flutter from tussock and bush. Snipe haunt the bogs. The dippers flit from stone to stone along the streams, and so do the wagtails, both pied and yellow. With luck one might see a pair of ring-ouzels now and again.

Grandest of all to see are the hawks that soar in the sky above and quarter to the moor from on high. Of these it is the buzzard that is most truly the bird of the moor. Seldom is the windy sky without one or a pair of these fine big hawks, their blunt wings spread wide as they plane with wonderful and effortless grace upon the air currents, their peculiar mewing cry carrying over the waste. Hovering kestrels may be seen suspended in the sky, and sometimes one may catch the bluey flash of a merlin's wing as this smallest of hawks rises from the heather. Marsh harriers come occasionally, and peregrines, and sometimes rarer hawks than these.

Another predatory bird – if so one may call it – which haunts the Hill is the raven. Ravens are far from scarce on Exmoor, and there are few days when I do not hear their horrid croak overhead. There is I think a resident pair hereabouts, but where they nest I have not yet discovered.

Of lesser creatures, the adder or viper has to be looked out for. These live up on the Hill, and not so very long ago a friend's dog was bitten and its life only saved with difficulty. But I must in all honesty confess I have not seen one myself for the past fifteen years or so. They must be very shy, or myself unobservant.

Insects of all sorts abound, but I am not an entomologist and know little of them, recognising only the more obvious sorts – the lovely brown butterflies which shimmer above the shining grasses in July (fritillaries of some kind), the larger moths that fly in the summer dusk, and a particular large black beetle which stumbles laboriously about and which has sapphire-blue legs and underparts.

All around there is life, the web of life of the wild hill, so much more than I can grasp, from the grazing beasts to the tiny lichens and fungi that sprout with the summer rain. One could spend forever contemplating it.

Whenever I come down off the Hill to the village again, I look always back upon the moor before I finally leave it. Its hills and combes swell and fall like the billows of the sea, and there is something inscrutable about it, timeless, changeless and indifferent to the haste of man. In its very wind-lashed heights and water-worn contours, moulded by the storms of ages, there is repose, the peace that comes out of elemental strife, the harmony that is cosmic.

Of the combes of the Hill, Knighton is my favourite. The other waters that flow away from the high ground are somewhat featureless – Dillacombe is a plain rough little valley, Westwater flows soon into enclosures, and the Halsecombe stream runs wholly outside the parish – but Knighton Combe is as beautiful as any upon Exmoor. It is near at hand too, for it comes down not half a mile from here. If one turns across the moor just where the moor begins, by the grassy stretch known as Waterhouse Green, one may discern a track of sorts leading through thickets of gorse into the combe. Mud at first, then stony washout comprise this "road" that was once the highway to Knighton farm. One comes down into the combe at a spot where there are green fields on the lower side, a pretty little wood of intermingled fir, larch and beech just opposite, and steep fern-covered cleeves reaching away upwards. So warm and sheltered it is here at all times, out of the buffeting winds, and the little stream runs gay over its stones. Under the trees, across a small fording place, there is set a gate, which is Combe Gate, the entry to Knighton fields. This spot here is interesting, for long before I knew much about it I had the feeling of habitation here. Then later I was told by someone who remembers much, that once there was a little holding just here. So I explored further, and sure enough just inside the gate, to the left under the trees and brush, I found the remains of old crumbling walls. Also, in the adjoining field I noticed that the remnants of a small low tin-roofed linhay had once been a building with at least one rounded pillar. Now upon the tithe map I see the dwelling house plainly marked where are the walls in the wood. So here was once somebody's holding, a small corner reft from the moor with labour and hope and faith in life. When did it go down, and why? No-one seems to know, or even remember its name.

My favourite sitting place in the combe is a short way upstream, where another narrower path comes to the water, finds a crossing place, and goes on thread-like up the far hillside. Slin's Path I am told it is called, and it is a "back door" to Knighton, going in to the fields somewhere at the top. Here is as much of earthly paradise as one may have on a sunny afternoon. The stream comes down most prettily over shelves of rock and chatters to itself about the scattered boulders. Thickets of gorse press down to the margin on this side – the scent of the massed yellow bloom on a warm May day is almost intoxicating – and a scattering of rowan trees fringe the stream where there is rooting place amongst the rocks. On the far side there are small lawns of close sheep-bitten turf like little green islands amongst the fern. Beyond and upwards the steep fern-covered, thorn-dotted hillsides close the view, beast-red at this time of year, sodden with winter rain.

It is a good spot to sit at ease in the comfort of winter sunshine and consider the history of the common, as much as is known of it, and the part it has played in the lives of folk, and man's own influence upon it.

High on the hills are the barrows, the earliest works of man, his first enduring marks upon the land. There is one on the summit of Withypool Hill itself and two on Brightworthy Hill – hence the hill itself is often called Brightworthy Barrows – another that is Green Barrow above the head of Knighton Combe, yet another on Bradymoor, and possibly there were others now lost upon the enclosed hills. They are all round barrows, the work of the Bronze Age folk who came this way sometime soon after 1800 BC. These folk of so long ago seem to have been nomadic pastoralists for there do not exist hereabouts any comparable hut circles such as would indicate settled existence. Most probably they lived much as Red Indians[11] of the prairie or the Mongols of the steppe did until recently, dwelling in tents, moving with the seasons, and coming together for religious or social ceremonies.

The land hereabouts must have looked much the same as does the combe and hill today, a waste of healthy ground rising high and open above the then impenetrable forest that cloaked all of the lower ground. Only with the difference, I think, that there would have been a lot more scrub clothing the slopes – there would be today if constant burning did not destroy the thorn, rowan and sallow that still tries to grow upon the hillsides.

One other monument these nameless pastoral folk have left us upon the moor, and that is the circle of stones that lies upon the west slope of Withypool Hill. If you would find it you must go up to the Hill-barrow, take a line on Porchester Post, and then walk downwards looking a little to the left. If the heather is low, fresh-burnt, you will see it easily, but not so easily if the growth has got high. The circle is about 40 paces across and some 29 stones still remain, most of them about knee-high.[12] You can sit in the middle in the sun when the wind is not too strong and look at the view, and muse for as long as you like upon the now forgotten people who came this way and raised this mysterious circle, and wonder what

[11] This is the term that Hope used. As editor I did consider changing it. However, this book is a period piece and Hope was using a term that was commonly accepted in the late 1960s. To change it would change the character and tone of Hope's work so I made the decision to let it stand, with this explanation.

[12] Hope was unsure of either the size of the circle or the number of stones remaining. This information was taken from ENPHER. The reference to 29 stones comes from a 1965 source.

strange ceremonies they held here and what their lives, so far from our own, were like.

The succeeding Celts have left no handiwork upon the Hill nor in the parish generally – unless it was they who first began to clear the scrub and found small farmsteads amongst the wood and waste. One wonders sometimes if some of our farms may not have been their work in the beginning. The pattern of small fields seems a Celtic one.

It is with the coming of the Saxons however that the founding of most of the farms, the enclosure of much of the land, and the growth of the customs of the Hill and parish may be said to begin. From these distant times of general settlement, more than a thousand years ago, come the traditional common rights, swaling customs and all other things that have obtained "since the memory of man runneth not to the contrary".

For a while, as mentioned, the parish of Withypool, fields and common alike, were held within the Royal Forest, but after the disafforestation of 1279 things returned to what was the normal manorial pattern of mediaeval England. So far as can be sorted out, most of Withypool and the whole of its common lay within the manor of Landacre, sometimes known as Withypool Suis and sometimes by some other appellations. To Landacre the common as such still belongs.

Common rights were, and still are, held by almost all the ancient "tenements" of the parish. These rights have always been highly valued, being an essential part of the hill-country economy, and jealously guarded. They have always been traditional, recognised by custom, and prevailing by common consent. In general the rights may be said to have consisted, from as far back as memory goes, of three primary things: the right of grazing, generally accepted as to be for as many sheep and cattle as a man might over-winter on his own land, plus ponies; the right to cut peat (turbary) enough for the hearth fire; and the right to cut fern and rush for bedding and thatching. From this one can see just how important these rights were to the hill farmer, particularly the small one, for they gave him extensive summer grazing for his beasts, allowing him to run his fields for hay in these months, they gave him fuel for his cooking fire, plus the ash for a spring fertilizer, and they gave him also a useful addition to his home-grown straw.

Until the Law of Property Act of 1922 put an end to copyhold, the affairs of manor and common were presided over the by the Court Leet, which as already mentioned was held every three years at either the house of the Lord of the Manor or at the Royal Oak inn. All matters concerning the common and its management were discussed and settled then. Some extra rights seem to have been allowed, such as the carting away of stone, and the diverting of water, but they had to be paid for. In olden times an official known as the portreeve seems to have watched over the common, or at least looked to the goings-on to see that proper rights were not exceeded.

Subsequent to 1922 affairs of the Hill went on without any proper management, and the result was that the common began to suffer from overstocking. More beasts were turned out than the ground could properly carry, breeds strange to the region were introduced, and it became usual to leave both sheep and cattle out all the year round, whereas previously it had been the custom to clear the Hill – except for the ponies – from November until the beginning of May. Also much indiscriminate burning or swaling took place. So in 1949 the Commoner's Association was formed by the commoners themselves, in an attempt to set forth principles and rules of stockings etc. which should be beneficial and fair to all.

The present stocking rates are fixed (I think) on an allowance, for summer grazing, of two sheep to the acre of the holder's in-ground, less that held for bullocks or ponies at the rate of four sheep to a beast, and for winter grazing half that number. Neither turf (peat) nor fern is cut any more – the last farm to cut rushes for thatching corn ricks was Higher Blackland, which maintained the practice until the late 1950s.

The old breeds that grazed the hill were those native to the region: the small hardy Exmoor Horn sheep, and the Devon Closewool, the red Devon cattle, and the native Exmoor ponies. In recent years all manner of outside breeds have been introduced and tried on the moor, and I have seen all sorts: of sheep, Swaledale, Scotch Blackface, Welsh Mountain, Clun, Kerry Hill, and every sort of half-breed imaginable; and of cattle, Shorthorn, Galloway, Belted Galloway, Friesian, and all sorts of in-betweens. Also some ponies of indeterminate breeding. Today however, the choice has narrowed again, and the sorts one mostly sees, in winter at least, are Scotch Blackface sheep, black Galloway cattle, plus a number of Devons and of course the Exmoor ponies.

Harking back to the nineteenth century, on two occasions Withypool almost lost its common. The first was in 1869 when it was proposed –and one presumes that this proposal was instigated by the larger landholders of the parish – to enclose the whole of the common. One acre only was to be left for "public recreation". Public opinion however was against it, and the bill did not get through Parliament. A second attempt was made in 1876, with ten and a half acres allowed for recreation etc., but again the scheme came to nothing. For this all of us who love the open moor must be devoutly thankful.

Round about this time, or beforehand, one or two people seem to have tried to "jump the gun" and to lay claim to bits of the common for themselves. There exists today one lonely enclosure right in the midst of the common, at the head of the Westwater stream, set like a small square island amidst the lapping heather. It is hedged in the traditional way and sub-divided into four small fields, from which it is known generally as "Four Fields". Its precise origin I do not know, but I have heard it called by another name – "Andrew's Platts" I think – and it a fair guess that someone of that name exercised "squatters rights" just here. Who he was, whether he had authority to enclose the land, or made any attempt to build a homestead here, no-one seems to remember. The bit of land is farmed from Willingford at the present.

Here and there one can trace what seem to be the remains of other banks upon the common, and likewise make a guess that unofficial enclosure of some sort was attempted from time to time in the past. Indeed I believe in the old days, in times of scarcity such as the Napoleonic wars, some temporary fencing-in of the more fertile patches was allowed, so that folk might grow a little extra corn for themselves, but the rule was that these plots had to be "let go" back to the moor at the end of three years. No doubt some folk attempted to hold on to such ground for as long as they could.

Roads over the moor were until fairly recently only rough unmetalled tracks. When a properly made-up road from North Molton was undertaken, the line first proposed was that of the track coming up from Willingford to Porchester's Post, and thence down into Withypool by Four Fields. Another branch was to go around the south side of the Hill proper to join the Hawkridge road near Greystone Gate. However, the route eventually fixed upon was that via Sandyway, which road is now our highway to the west, running from here to there by way of the rise known as Knowle's Heard and the little Portford Bridge that spans the southern stream-head of Knighton Combe, and so to Crooked Post.

The only other recent erections by man upon the common are the small and unobtrusive water catchment in the north branch of Knighton Combe (from which Withypool gets its water supply), and the ordnance stone upon the summit of Brightworthy Hill, the highest point in the parish.

Thinking some last thoughts about the Hill, and coming to some conclusions drawn from personal observation over many years, I am bound to say that I think the vegetation of the Hill is gradually becoming poorer. The heather is becoming less both in extent and vigour of growth, and is being replaced by coarse grasses. Whortleberry is much less than it used to be, and there are few good beds to pick from now. In many another way one notices this trend. The two principal causes of this are, I would say, too frequent burning of the heather – though swaling is one of the principles of management of heather-moor, heather is a very slow-growing shrub and can't stand it too often – and the winter stocking of the common with creatures other than ponies. With regard to the sheep especially, wintering stock pick every bud and blade that appears towards the spring, and nothing except what is really unpalatable ever gets a chance. In this matter the roving Blackface are probably the worst offenders. But I am not a commoner, so I suppose I have no right to either complain or offer advice.

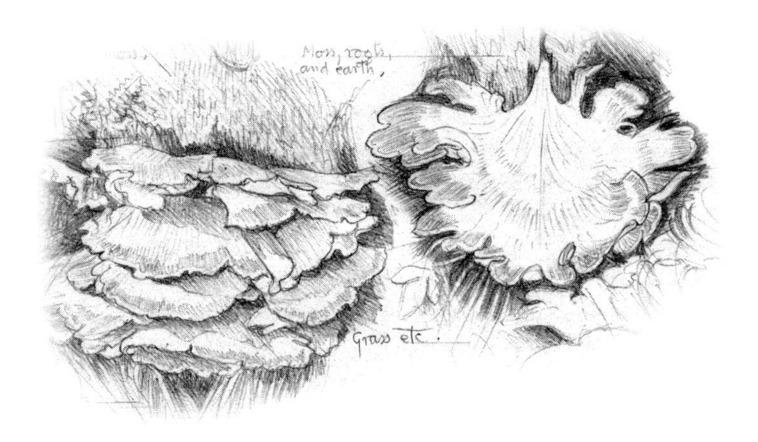

CHAPTER FIVE

A Walk Around the Bounds of the Parish

A walk round the bounds of the parish is good exercise on a fine day – or any other day for that matter – for it will take one for some eleven miles through fields, woods and combes, over the Hill and down to the river, and give one a fair view of all the country within the parish, and the nature of it, and also glimpses of the four adjoining parishes.

Comer's Gate is as good a starting point as any, so up the hill to Comer's Cross. Across the small lower Pennycombe Bridge, with a glance upstream at the clattering water where it runs under a knot of firs and beech, and downwards to the big river under the tall water-poplars, and here, just beside, is Garliscombe, or what is left of it. A few small buildings round a tiny yard on one side of the road, and some sheds on the other – the remains of what was once a small farm, an ancient one owing one suit on the older suitor's list. The sheds on the right hand comprise the remnants of the house, and seem locally to have acquired the name of "Rat's Castle" – probably with good reason. Anciently, the highway must have run right through the yard, but since the only traffic would have been an occasional horseman, this would have meant little.

The road ascends steeply up a hill marked on-in-five, but which is almost certainly steeper than that in the middle. It curves around the shoulder of the hill, and half-way up there is a good vantage point for a view over the valley and back to the village clustered under the dark moor. Coming downwards, though, this main road into Withypool – known as Quarry Head, on account of its having some one-time quarry pits on its flank – does not offer an altogether pleasing view for drivers not accustomed to it, for the combination of gradient, curve, and giddy drop on the outside, is apt to be unnerving, especially in icy weather. (There was one winter occasion, back in the days when we had buses, when the bus got into difficulties on the ice-covered surface here, and both driver and passengers had some nasty moments. However, all eventually arrived safely at the bottom of the road). On the left hand side as one ascends one passes the gates of the two "big houses" standing above, and one gateway through which some sheds may be seen, which marks the site of Sweetwalls, another little ancient farm like Garliscombe, now quite gone. The rough banks hereabouts are bright with daffodils in the spring, but they are planted ones, not wild. The entry to Uppington farm lies on the right.

Now here is Comer's Cross, a wide crossways on the Dulverton road, and to the right, about a hundred yards off, is Comer's Gate.

Many memories I have as I stand here at Comer's Gate and look southward over the big sweep of moorland which is Winsford Hill. Memories of many meets of the staghounds, when all roads, verges and this end of the moor are thronged with horsemen and jammed with cars and boxes, and the morning is filled with excitement, and the hounds are drawn up under the hedge just to the left, and the red coats make a splash of glorious colour against the waste of fern and heather. Memories too, of deer crossing the hill in twilight, coming up from the tangled Winbrook to go over to the covert of the Barle. All this and so much more.

Turn again and face north-westwards, come again to the crossroads, and set off along the main road to Exford. All within the circuit now, to one's left hand, is Withypool, whilst that outside, upon the right hand, is of other parishes.

For a little while one must walk upon the main road, but it is the only stretch in the circuit, and there is not much traffic in the winter. Away to the east, at the bottom of Ash Lane, lies Winsford, and Winsford parish borders here for a way. Two fields from the cross on the Winsford side, Room Hill, another expanse of rough moor, falls away to the Exe. Below is one of the wilder stretches of the Exe valley, all precipitous cleaves, scarped rocks, and wet scrub woods, the whole matted with fern and haunted by deer. (Once, not so very long ago, that is, within living memory, it was the haunt also of a race of wild cats, possibly the last remnant of *Felix silvestris* to survive in the west of England. But they have gone this past fifty years).[13] Two very ancient farms, Nethercote and Lyncombe, and also Lyncombe packhorse bridge, lie in the valley, but they hardly concern a dissertation on Withypool.

Room Hill is bounded from the road by a hedge, and there are fields – those of the Weatherslade farm – on the other side, but the Ordnance map of 1809 shows all this high ground (the whole of which is properly Room Hill) as open moorland. The enclosure must have been made sometime between then and 1839, as the tithe map gives fenced fields along most the left-hand side.

This stretch of road is high and wide, and shows in this its recent origin, being in great contrast to the narrow sunken lanes that are the oldest highways between farm and farm. As a moorland trackway though, it was probably very ancient, almost certainly being a prehistoric hill route. The views, where one can see over or between the beech hedging, are wide, from Dunkery to Exe Head. The metalled roadway I remember as being much narrower, barely more than wide enough for one car's width, and flanked all along by wide grass verges upon which one could canter a horse in comfort from Comer's Gate to Chibbet Post. But that was fifteen years ago, and motor traffic is the god of the present. Other more recent memories of this particular stretch of the road I have too, of snow in 1963, but that belongs to a chapter on its own.

Somewhat before reaching the fork with the lower road, the boundary turns sharply west, along the edge of the Foxtwitchen fields. All now on the outside is Exford parish. On the inside the angle of land is shown as rough moorland on the tithe map, though it is now fields. The said boundary now crosses the Halsgrove Land, runs between the Halsgrove and Buckworthy fields, and plunges into Pennycombe.

Down a little rough goyle, over some squelching rush, and one is by Pennycombe Water, all racing and sparkling on its way down to the big river. Tall steep fern and gorse-covered cleaves tower all around, shutting out the wider world, and mats of wood cling to their sides, whilst rush beds fill the floor. Upstream there are wild outcrops of rock, and downstream old mining tunnels penetrating far into the hillsides – but Pennycombe must have a chapter to itself.

Chibbet Ford, however, I feel I must mention here, for it is a little way upwards and just outside the parish, but it is a spot dear to me, for I lived there once, for a while, at one of the cottages. If one goes on up a little

[13] In Hope's personal collection of books there is a copy of *Lost Beasts of Britain*, by Anthony Dent (1974). In this text (p. 88) he recounts stories of wild cats in a "region of West Somerset which is to this day one of the only two habitats in England of the wild red deer". Dent goes on to say that children about Withypool were warned to go inside the house if one of these wild cats approached the farmyard.

way, scrambling over the rocky steps whereabouts in late May are carpets of bluebells, one comes to a place where a road descends sharply to the stream and crosses it by a shallow ford. Here are three cottages set under the rocks, and a little stone-slab footbridge and white ducks upon the water. Dear Chibbet Ford, it was from here that I first knew Withypool and stepped forth to explore the district, many, many years ago.

Climbing up out of Pennycombe – not an easy passage – one looks back over Buckworthy (in Exford) and sees its low white farmhouse, and newer buildings set in smooth green fields above the combe. One is now on Blackland territory – fields I know oh, so well, for the farm above was home to me for many years – and the boundary runs right up to Higher Blackland Farm. Here it turns away westwards, running straight along the spine of Blackland Hill to Bradymoor Gate with enclosures on both sides. The fields on the inside are ancient, but all the land upon the outside was until 1852 open moor, being Exford South Common. The big rectangular enclosures now here tell their own story, being in marked contrast to the irregular smaller older fields of the farm. (Though of another parish, large portions of this common seem to have been granted to Higher and Lower Blackland, and also to Landacre).

A "green lane", a droveway to the moor, runs parallel to the parish bounds on the inside, from Higher Blackland farm to Bradymoor Gate, and for mud, real deep squelching, holding clinging mud, I have seldom known its equal. It is better to proceed along this stretch by turning through the first gate on the left and following the line of gateways through sunny fields to the point where the line eventually emerges from its tunnel of hedges to become a length of hardened track along the top of the moor.

Here at last is the open moor. The hedges fall away, the wide expanse of heather and bent and rush stretches from one's feet into seeming infinity, the distant hilltops float in light and seem to beckon, and one knows such a feeling of freedom and release as is not to be found in any confined space, however beautiful. Here is the wild land, the primaeval, the untamed, and it calls to one's soul. Day and night I have known this stretch of moor that opens here, Bradymoor it is called, and I think more of my being is bound here than in any other place.

Turn and face the sun, and here immediately before one is Bradymoor Bog, its rush pools glittering like fragments of mirror in the light. Here in the spring the frogs croak and the snipe drum, and there are small strange plants amongst the sphagnum moss. At one's back is the hedge bank of Blackland Allotments, and a hundred yards further on is Bradymoor Gate spanning the road to Landacre, that is the Exford-North Molton road. Hence the next five miles are all over open moor.

Bradymoor Gate is a grid today, as are most "Gates" nowadays, all smartly painted black-and-white, but once it was a horseman's gate across a moorland track and clacked with a wooden latch. Bradymoor Gate! Still it is a favourite meet of the Exmoor Foxhounds, and so often I have waited here and seen the riders gather and mill, and then the pack and the red coats come streaming along the track under the hedge from Simonsbath. And watched them too throw off across the bog, and waited so eagerly for a find in the rushes.

Here also is – or was – the County Library van's stop for Higher Blackland, and so I know it doubly well. Often I have crouched under a hedge with an armful of books, swathed in waterproofing, trying to evade the worst of the wind and driving rain, and straining my ears for the sound of the heavy van coming up the hill from Chibbet Ford! Hunting mornings, or library mornings, Bradymoor Gate is a wild enough place on a stormy winter's day.

The hedge on the other side of the Gate makes a jutting angle, and then runs westward in a long straight line. Here now under one's feet and stretching away to the south and west is thick heather moor. There is a track of sorts along under the hedge, but it is so squelchy and rutted that it is better to keep to the heather and stride over the dark tussocky bush. The long hedge bank itself is the parish boundary, with various Exford enclosures on the north side, and it runs on for more than a mile in a dead straight line. Most of the beech is laid now, but it used to be a huge wind-battered stand, breaking the force of the gales, and very picturesque to draw or paint, as I have so often done, sitting in the deep heather. The view away to the south-west is free and wide, right to Five Barrows over in Devon, and this is a part of the moor I love. Halfway along a single tree stands out, and under its boughs is Gipsy Lane Gate, a gateway giving access to a rough track leading away towards Honeymead. Presently one comes to another area of bog, all treacherous with black peat hags and difficult to bypass even keeping close to the hedge. Pickedstones Bog – it is a nasty place, especially if one is riding.

Now before one, having passed the bog, is a hedge at right-angles, running south, and in the corner a gate, a glimpse of tarmac, and another grid a few yards on. Pickedstones Gate, and the metalled road leading downwards to Pickedstones Farm and outwards to Honeymead and Simonsbath. Here now one is come to the bounds of the ancient Forest. Here end both the parishes of Withypool and Exford, and here, until the Disafforestation Act of 1815, all beyond was one vast tract of treeless, unenclosed, uninhabited moorland. (That is, with the sole exception of Simonsbath House, which had been built in the heart of the Forest in the seventeenth century). Pickedstones and all the other farms that one can glimpse are the creations of less than 150 years. Today all this ground constitutes the parish of Simonsbath, and it is by Simonsbath that we turn down along the southern-running hedge to the river. Three-quarters of the way down a green track comes through red fern beds to a gate and goes away through Pickedstones enclosure – the old riding track from Withypool into the Forest and down to Horsen Ford. (The branch running on to Simonsbath itself passed, I think, higher up, nearer Pickedstones, to go by the White Water ford and up through Winstitchen).

Here now is the river, the Barle, in its own wild valley, coming down broad and strong from even wilder reaches high in the Forest, past the great craggy outcrop of Cow Castle, to join before one's feet with Sherdon Water, and to flow with the latter into a big deep wide pool. Sherdon Pool is well known to the young folk for miles around, being a favourite bathing place on hot summer days, and in its clear cool water many have learned to swim. I have memories of the bite of its water on a July afternoon, picnics on the banks, and cricket on a patch of smooth sward near to hand! Just below the pool is a ford, used by horsemen, and once, I am told, by horses and carts coming or going between Pickedstones farm and North Molton. (What a struggle either way, up the steep moor tracks!) The parish bounds cross the river here, but the ford is too deep and strong for travellers on foot to pass over – except in times of dry summer, when it runs shallow – so one must either digress downstream to Landacre Bridge, or else go home and come another day upon the other side.

Once one is upon the other side, here again at the junction of waters known as Sherdon Hutch, one walks for a few yards up Sherdon Water, and then turns up the hill, crossing the old Ferny Ball track, to come to Kingsland Pits. Ferny Ball, across the stream, makes me feel sad. Once it was a cosy farm, set in a fold between Ferny Ball hill and Great Sherdon, full of sunshine. I came here once, riding on a newly-broken Exmoor pony, proud to show-off the pony to the friends who lived here, and remember the welcome and the sunlight, and the exhilaration of the ride across the moor. A short while after this the place was burnt to the ground – an accident with an oil heater late one night – and was never re-built though I don't know why. The land passed to another farm, and what was left of the house – the shell of the ground floor – was roofed as a storage shed. So passed an Exmoor farm, which, though not so very ancient, and outside the parish – being within the Forest – was on the Withypool postal round, and so considered locally to be part of Withypool.

Kingsland Pits, rocky hollows in the hillside, appear to be of natural origin, though some road-metal may have been drawn out of them when either the track below or the road above was surfaced. Just below here one branch of the track goes on to Lower Sherdon, another Forest farm, one set halfway up the face of Sherdon Hill. The boundary hedge passes just to the south west of the Pits.

Now here is the road coming up from Landacre Bridge, and another grid, this one known generally as Lower Muddy Lane Gate. Over the road, and along one goes under the hedge of Landacre Allotments, taking care, as this part of the route is somewhat squelchy – the cotton grass waves white here in June – and so one passes over the high western shoulder of Withypool Common to the Withypool-North Molton Road and yet another grid. This one is Muddy Lane Gate proper (a nice commentary on the state of the roads hereabouts before someone invented tarmac), and here the hedge turns sharp left and runs parallel with the road for a way, but just here the actual boundary makes an inward swing before rejoining the road, leaving a small half-moon of moor ground betwixt, which is labelled Hawkridge Common. The why or wherefore of this I do not know, but the land on the south side of the hedge – Halscombe allotment – is in the Hawkridge parish, and so this bit seems to have got left out at the time of the enclosure of the latter. The road itself goes on to join the Exford one about a mile further on at what is now generally known as Withypool Cross, but was anciently called Crooked Post, and thence by Sandyway to the lower country.

The Withypool bounds touch Green Barrow, sunk and crumbling in the rushes, and then swing in to the corner of the Halscombe Allotment fence where it turns south-east to Porchester Post. The Allotment is still an area of rough moor, and follows along until the old lane comes up from Willingford to the gate upon Withypool Common which is called Porchester's Post – from the custom, I believe, of the late Lord Porchester holding frequent meets of his hounds here – and at this point the bounds reach their southernmost extent.

Willingford down the lane is one of the loneliest of farms, for there is still no proper road approach, though there is a pretty little bridge in the bottom, from which a track continues to White Post. This is the way to Cussacombe, from Withypool, moor all the way (for the lane though fenced, is flanked all its length by rough ground, until it debouches on Molland Moor), and this is the way the Staghounds go, coming up the rutty peaty track over Withypool Hill, when the meet is Cussacombe Post. It is a walk or ride which I love.

The scenery of this last stretch is of deep woods coming down close to the water, shutting one in with the river-sound until one turns up and away to the top of the Ham – but the description belongs properly to another chapter. Once upon the top one is in the big enclosures of the Ham, until recently all thick fern, and not ploughed out until a few years ago. For the last quarter mile the boundary abuts on Winsford Hill, and then, at last, one is back to Comer's Gate whence one started. So one has circumnavigated one's parish, and though this may seem to signify little in this modern age, yet I confess I have done so with a certain sense of personal possession. In some way this territory is mine, and belongs to me, even though I do not own an acre of it.

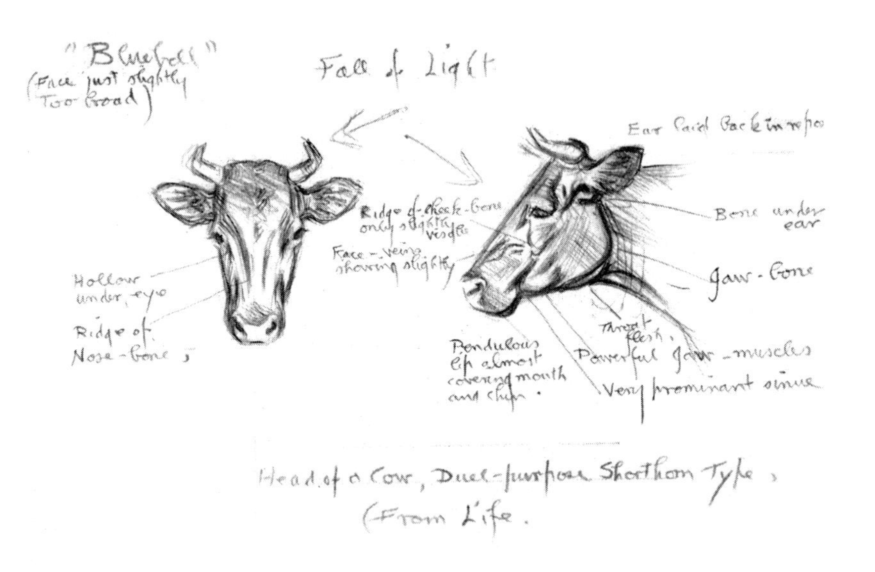

CHAPTER SIX

The River Upwards

If one stands upon Withypool Bridge and looks upstream, one sees before one a pleasant vista of broad bright water and reed-fringed banks, with small fields and bushy hedges coming close, and a tall poplar tree to mark the view like an asterisk. Beyond, to close the immediate scene, and to hint at the wilderness of the upper reaches, is the big shoulder of Brightworthy Hill, field-hedges climbing up as far as they dare, but the top defiantly free and brown with tawny moor. It is a view that I always linger to look at as I cross the bridge.

There was here, before the bridge was built about a hundred years ago, a ford – it is so marked on the old tithe map – and there still is access to the river at three corners of the bridge. The broadest of these is at the south-west butt, where there is a wide patch of grass and a shallow way down to the water. Just here the foxhounds (the Dulverton West) meet in winter, the red coats bright against the grey stone of the bridge, whilst in summer young folk ride their ponies into the water for a splash.

Just behind, as one stands or sits on the grass here, is one of the prettiest features of Withypool, which one must needs turn round and look at – a little fenced enclosure planted with rowan trees. The planting was made, I believe, to commemorate the Coronation of 1953, and was a happy thought, for these little trees, so essentially trees of the moor and mountain, are a joy at all times, silvery-branched in winter, laden with creamy white flowers in early summer, glorious with blood-red berries in later summer, and finally ablaze with red and russet leaves in the autumn. There is one tree especially which sheds the reddest and most perfect leaves of its kind I have ever seen. I look for these leaves as they come down in October, for they are gems more beautiful than the artifices of any jeweller, and take one or two to lay on my table each day, though they soon wither indoors.

Here too is the first of the Hill cattle grids with its attendant gates all painted white. It is the barrier to the grazing beasts of the moor, so that they shall not come down into the village proper. In winter both sheep and cattle come down this far, and lurk around the gardens and enclosures on the Hill side, but never the ponies – they are too shy.

A footpath leads for a way along the south bank, and about a hundred yards along one comes to the site of the old bridge just under the poplar tree. The butt is still visible on the opposite side, and behind one is the short length of green-gated lane which was once the highway leading to it. What this original bridge was like, and when it was built one can only guess. Probably it resembled Landacre, and likewise originated in the later Middle Ages. It would have been narrower, for the river narrows in here, which was probably the reason for the old bridge being built here in the first instance.

In the angle between the green lane, the present road, and the river bank lay anciently the Forest Pound, the enclosure into which unauthorised animals found straying upon the Forest were brought by the foresters or other officials. Here the owners might claim them upon payment, or if unclaimed they became forfeit to the chief forester as estrays.

Small enclosures come down to the river on both sides, and those that lie on the south bank are known as the Parish Gardens, though I don't know why. A little further along a piece of overgrown laneway appears by the river, seemingly coming from nowhere and going nowhere, but on looking around one sees to one side a heap of bramble-covered stones which are obviously the remains of walls. Here once was a little homestead, someone's little cot set between the moor and the river. Its name appears to be Langwalls, and its life-span short for it is not marked on the tithe map, so must have been built since, and it has been gone down a long time now.[14]

[14] The 1905 6" OS map of Withypool shows a building called "Langs" around this spot.

The first farm on this side of the river is Waterhouse. It is a small farm of about forty acres, its fields running narrowly between the moor and the river. Its buildings group tightly about the yard, but as the house is set on the south side, that is, with its back to the yard, one may gather that neither is the house very old nor the site original. One would have to look somewhere on the other side of the yard for the remains of the older farmhouse.

Across the river and slightly higher up is Newland Farm. It is sited fairly low near the river, sitting in the sun and out of the wind, but its land runs right up over Kitridge Hill, 1100 feet at the top. High, sunny and breezy are its fields as I know well, for I have often sat in them and sketched the views over valley and moor. I have not been into the yard now for several years, since the friends I had there left, but as I remember it, the house faced south into the yard with a small walled garden before it, and the main range of building flanked it to face east. Of course it must still do, but I think there have been some alterations. The house was – or is – plainly built, and although in the appropriate position for an old house yet in fact it is not so. The original house was set facing east, in alignment with the buildings, and it is so shown on the tithe map. This siting is corroborated by the existence of some ruins of sorts visible at the back of the present house, which to me looked like the remains of an older house.

The west end of the house would however seem to incorporate some part of an older building, for if I remember correctly, there is a ceiling of fine chamfered beams in the sitting room on that side. The farm itself was once a place of substance and some importance, for in the past century the Notleys, Lords of the Manor, resided here. Its "suit" was three in the old suitor's lists, denoting it to be a large holding. Also, its large acreage is now reduced to a very few fields, the land having been sold off and the place now a private residence. The name "Newland" takes one back many centuries to far distant days when the farm was new and its land new-taken from the wild. "La Nywelond" it was in the archaic spelling of 1270, and had probably been so for a long time then.

The chief feature of the farm – from the point of interest in local architecture – was the presence, just outside the main yard, of a fine old round-pillared cart linney. I remember it well, for I made several sketches of it. Four big drum pillars held up the old slate roof, each of perfectly round ragstone masonry, and there were still carts and the remains of carts amongst the nettles within. Alas, it was already on the way to becoming a ruin when I knew it, with slates slipping off the roof and ivy climbing over the gables, so I expect it will have tumbled down, or been pulled down, by now. Which is a great pity, for it was in its simple way a noble building, with dignity in its form and purpose, and the best of its kind I know. It was in itself a monument to the local building tradition, for these old round-pillared standings were once common to the Exmoor country, chiefly I would guess because of the difficulty of bonding the local rag or rubble in a squared column, though an additional reason would be the greater ease of manoeuvring a cart about a rounded pillar. There are still several others of this sort, though smaller, in the district, but such as still stand tend to be converted into sheds. The main reason for their demise is that the space between the pillars is generally too narrow for modern machinery.

Below the farm a piece of laneway leads to a ford providing a crossing to Waterhouse or perhaps one should say did, for the great flood of 1952 scoured the riverbed hereabouts so much that the ford is no longer used even by hunting folk.

Westwards another lane runs along by the water meadows that here shelve out under the hill, and comes to the shoulder of Newland Wood and the old ford to Brightworthy. Once this would have been the highway to Brightworthy Farm on the far hill, but now it is never used, and the gates are fastened up and the old lane all clogged with fallen branches from the scrubby hillside. One comes to the riverbank, if one picks one's way down the muddy-bottomed lane, just under the big precipitous bluff of Newland Wood. Here is a spot which seems always to me to hold a curious atmosphere, a sense of mystery or foreboding, I know not why. The water before one is broad and sunny, and upon the far banks is the gate leading up from the ford to Knighton and Brightworthy Meadows. The scene is fair enough, though I would not like to try the ford even on horseback, for it looks deep and uncertain, at least at this time of year. Over one's shoulder, though, the mass of Newland Wood crowds down to the water with a dark and brooding effect. The cliff-like bluff which it clothes juts here right to the river's edge, cutting off further progress westwards, and then curves backwards in a half-moon shape, holding within and beneath itself a mysterious and seemingly unapproachable patch of rush-grown mead. One day, scrambling around in an adventurous mood, I discovered an ancient pathway around the bluff. It was all overgrown and hidden under fallen branches, and I had to pick my way with care, but there it was, amazingly cut through the living rock, just wide enough for man and beast to traverse in single file, and leading into the mysterious mead. How old was it? Who in past centuries had thought the rushy wet mead worth the labour of cutting a rock-path to it? Perhaps the same hands had attempted to drain the mead. Certainly this half-moon shape of ground facing the sun would have held the noon-day warmth like a bowl, and shut off from all cold winds and with the dampness of the river, it might have produced, with good drainage, the lushest of grazing. But why then was it abandoned? Today there is only rush and sallow bush, and a sense of desolation. Yet once, I feel, there were buildings of some sort back against the dark foot of the wood. It is of course only imagination, yet the feeling is always with me.

Upon the top of Kitridge Hill the scene is different. Here there is wind and wide views, and open fields. One is above the wood, and one's feelings those of exhilaration. Hereabouts is a spot which is one of my favourites, one where I come often to sit at all times of the year, and at all hours. It is just above the top of the wood, sheltered by the curve of a hedge from the winds of the north and east, and holding the sun from mid-morning to sunset. As I sit here, reclining against the sunny bank, I look upon a splendid view. Before me is the westwards valley of the Barle seen through the treetops, and below, flowing from the Forest, the river winding as a ribbon of blue-grey between the hills. Ferny scarps, meads, green fields and tawny moor all intermingle in a great harmony, with here and there a white- washed farmhouse showing above a knot of trees, and far off to close the view the distant blue line of the Fyldon Ridge and Span Head. So often I have sat here, in summer and in winter, in the morning when the sun is on the hills, and in the evenings when the hills are turned to shadowy blue and the river a highway of golden light down the valley sunk in mystery. I have sat here in deep snow, with all the world before me turned to a dazzling white shadowed with purest ultramarine under a sky of china blue, and been as warm in the sun as on a summer's day, and felt the land to be enchanted.

Looking back across the valley, I can see the two farms of Knighton and Brightworthy spread out on their hillsides like maps. The pattern is interesting. Brightworthy lies high and dry across a ball of hill and its land sunny and well-drained between the bogs of the moor which lie at the back and the cleaves and meads which lie at its feet. Knighton, which fills the space between the former and Waterhouse, spreads out on a lower, shallower slope, parts of its land still considerably rushy despite modern improvement. Here one sees the natural differences which have made the distinction between what has always been considered a good farm and one that has been less good and subject to fluke.

It is however, the actual pattern of the enclosures that intrigues me as I sit looking across from my high place, especially those of Brightworthy. All the land here is contained in a big ring-hedge which makes an irregular circle upon the hill, and within this the ground is subdivided into numerous and more-or-less rectangular fields. Obviously all the land here was taken in from the moor all at one time and then afterwards laid out in fields, not the reverse, that is, the in-ground being added to a few fields at a time through the centuries. How long, how very long ago was this big encircling hedge-topped boundary bank thrown up? Seven hundred, a thousand years ago? Perhaps more? It is impossible to say, but here surely is the ancient "outfield" system of taking-in land from the wild in one lump, and afterwards breaking it up piecemeal, which is believed to be of Celtic origin. The only guess is that Brightworthy must be a very ancient farm indeed.

As it stands, Knighton is the most interesting farmstead of the two – or was until a short while ago, for it has been much altered in the past few years. When I first knew it its only approach was a very narrow muddy rutty track of a lane coming in from Combe Gate in Knighton Combe and ending in the rough-floored yard through which flowed the water-splat from the moor above. The house, facing east across the yard to the simple shippons, was then one of the oldest and least altered of its kind in the district. It was long and low, built of rough moor-stone, and the roof was thatched. There was a slope-roofed porch shielding an old black nail-studded door, and beside it a buttress which gave strength to the fabric and feature to the aspect. Under the parlour window there was a tiny flower-patch protected from the passing beasts by a "fence" of big upright-set slate slabs. The upper windows looked out from under the thatch like lidded eyes. Round at the back there were only blank walls, the sole feature being the abutment of the inner staircase. The chimneys arose from the gable-ends, and at the north end, continuing in a line with the house, was the cow shippon. Within, one entered through a screen passage of wall and timber into, on the left, the old stone-flagged open-hearthed kitchen, and, on the right, the smaller parlour. From the latter a cupboard door gave access to the twisting stair within the abutment, and above were several bedrooms opening one from the other. Once, I was told, there had been fine linen-fold panelling in the parlour, but this had long disappeared.

Though no definite history of the place seems recorded, I would myself say that as it stood then it was an almost unaltered sixteenth century farmhouse, possibly incorporating some older mediaeval work.

Reputedly it was haunted. Friends of mine, who lived and farmed there for many years, often told me of queer happenings that occurred such as things being moved out of place, or noises heard, without any rational cause or explanation. An older generation put this down to "pixies", and a more modern one to poltergeist manifestation.

For myself, I have never felt anything oppressive in the atmosphere of the place. For a number of years it was empty and deserted, no-one apparently wanting a place with so few modern amenities, and I often used to sit in the sunny overgrown yard and make sketches of the old place, and muse of its past, present, and possible future.

Now, however, all is altered, for the old farm has been reconditioned and is once again occupied. A new tarmac road runs in across the top from Portford, going right on through to Brightworthy, the yard is concreted, and the old house unrecognisable under a roof of modern composition and a facing of terracotta roughcast. Even the porch is gone, and the buttress. I am glad that the place is lived in and a home again, but sorry that something of the original character of the place could not have been preserved.

Brightworthy itself has little to show of antiquity. The house, a four-square building, stands apart from the yard, facing south-east up the hill, and cannot be very old. Possibly one might find indications of an older house if one explored the yard. Once, however, there seem to have been three dwellings, three holdings together here, for the oldest existing free suit list give four suits for the place, attaching respectively to Higher, Middle, and Lower Brightworthy. How long ago this sub-division might have existed, one can only guess. The place is a single farm on the tithe map. But I have, on occasion, noticed in the field to the south of the house, an unevenness of the ground which would seem to indicate the remains of banks and walls, so perhaps there was another farmstead here once. In a document of 1298 the place is "Briztenesworthy" and classed as a hamlet.

Until recently Brightworthy was the hardest of all the farms in the parish to get at, for it had no road approach of any sort and was parted from Knighton by a steep combe. The choice of ways of entry were across the river ford under Newland and up the meadows, in along the roughest of tracks over the moor from Landacre Bridge, or over the top of Brightworthy Hill from Green Barrow and down through rushy uncertain ground to the top fields. All of these ways were difficult in bad weather and rendered Brightworthy very much a world on its own. I well remember the farmer and his family, who lived there then, coming down to the Post Office on horseback each week to take back their groceries in saddle-bags. Later they had a Land Rover. Then, a few years ago the new road was made into Knighton, and this was engineered to span the intervening combe and go on into Brightworthy. So now Brightworthy has a road, but it was the last farm in the district to get this.

But to return to Newland Wood. The trees here are a mixture of oak and beech, with a fringe of ash, rowan and thorn. Thick and leafy in summer, gloriously russet in autumn, they are now bare-branched but hung about with festoons of pale grey-green "Spanish Moss". This strange damp-loving lichen (which seems to be of several sorts) clings everywhere here, hanging in beards, and covering some of the thorns so completely that they seem as ghostly shapes against the dark depths of the wood. If one ventures down into the wood, by a path that runs into it, one comes in the midst to a spring of fresh water breaking from the hill, and beside it pieces of crumbling wall. What was once here, all amongst the trees? The juxtaposition of springhead and walling suggest a dwelling, but who would want to live in the depths of shadowy wood? There is no memory by anybody of anything having ever been here, so it is just another little mystery. Perhaps by now the walling has quite crumbled away, for it is many years since I went down the under-path, for, once again, I do not care for the depths of Newland Wood. Much rather do I prefer the little cow-path along its upper fringe, bright and sunny and deep in fern, and, in early June, giving glimpses of Hillway ground. Hereabouts is another favourite spot of mine, just where the wood begins to fall away to the river, and there are open grassy slopes again. To sit here on a June evening, with the light shining through the young green-gold leaves of oak, ash and beech onto the greener grass is a dream-like experience.

Sometimes I go down to the river just here, slipping and sliding down a slope so steep that I never get to the bottom without at least one tumble. The valley here has a wild aspect, with the dark wood at one's back and the barer moor coming down to the brink upstream. One can, if one has a mind, scramble along under the wood to where the "hidden mead" begins at this end, but it is a soggy squelching walk amongst rushes and sallow bushes. The river at this reach makes great convolutions, looping back upon itself so as to create almost an island of a neck of the mead, and by throwing up big shelves of shingle, shows with what fury it tears down this valley in times of spate. There used to be a pool of great depth just hereabouts, so I am told, the deepest of all the Barle, and woe to the creature that ever fell in, but the great flood of 1952 filled it up a good deal, even as in reverse it scoured-out a lot of the fords.

The last time I came down here to the river, not very long ago, the river was running high, a steel-grey tide racing with breaks of foam between the topmost lips of the banks. I sat down on the brink for a little while, despite the spattering rain, before making the tough climb back up the hillside. Never had the scene been so impressive. Great dark storm clouds banked up from the west, undershot with lurid white-heads. The fern on the flats and scarps was sodden to a dark heavy red, the bare sallow-bushes turned to a stark black (is there anything blacker than sallow soaked by days of rain?) and the distant hills loomed a dull dark colour. Gusts of wind drove the rain into my eyes, but the river itself made little noise beyond a steady muttering, it running too deep to roar. Here to me was Exmoor, the true land, not the one of the bright picture-postcards beloved by tourists.

Upon the hill above is Hillway Farm, one which must surely have the finest views of any in the parish. It is a lovely little place, set on the rim of the steep, overlooking the valley with the command of a fort. But it is no fortress, but a neat sunny farmstead with whitewashed walls bright against a windbreak of beech and fir trees. The house faces due south into – or rather over, for it is set high – the narrow yard, and there is a barn jutting out at the west end. There used to be other buildings on the drop side where is now a terrace-like space, but most of these have been pulled down in recent years, a new block of modern buildings on higher ground taking their place. The old farm has perched here for a long time, for it is "Hyldeweys" in the records of 1270, and it must have seen many changes. The present owners have done much to improve it, including the making of a very pretty garden, through which tumbles the little splat of fresh water which comes down from the moor above. The whole place has a peculiar quality about it, as of quiet grace and pleasure. It satisfies. The farm, the fields in the sun, the grazing beasts, the comfortable house, the garden, the tall trees, the wide view over hill and valley, all combine to give a sense of balance and earthly goodness.

To the east of Hillway is a small combe, which is its boundary. Beyond is Landacre, farm, fields and bridge, but Landacre needs a chapter of its own, so this one must needs end here.

CHAPTER SEVEN

The River Downwards

Downstream from Withypool Bridge the river twists and turns through a narrowing valley enclosed with steep hills and cloaked with woods. Though Withypool Hill dominates the valley on one side and Winsford Hill on the other, broad stretches of farmland intervene between the open moor and the hanging woods, so that the valley hereabouts has less of a moorland character than in its upper reaches, and assumes more the aspect of "green country", an intermingling of field, mead and primaeval woodland. Here begin the deer coverts, the greatest in the country after Horner, which stretch almost unbroken down through Hawkridge to below Dulverton. It is country for a hot summer's day, or perhaps a wild windy one when one is glad to escape the buffeting on top.

There is a path if one wants to walk by the river, which begins by the rise of Quarry Head and then drops to follow the left bank, or one can potter along the Hawkridge road and the valley from above, dropping down to it when one wants to. Either way or according to mood, the scenery is fine.

A little way downstream from the bridge Pennycombe Water runs into the big river, and here upon a spit of ground at the junction is Barle Mill or Garliscombe Mill, the ancient water-mill which once ground the corn for the bread of Withypool. The line of the leat can still be marked, diverging from Pennycombe, and the skeleton of the waterwheel still remains, silent and unmoving now. The tall water-poplars shake their heads above, and remember other days.

Across the water is Kings, the first farm of this lower valley, set just beyond the knoll of beeches which make a feature of the view from the bridge, and upon the first big bend of the river. As a farm it is an ancient one, though small in acreage according to present day standards, but the house is large, and would seem to be mostly of fairly modern construction, though possibly incorporating some parts of older fabric. Probably that part of the house which faces south is the oldest, with the obviously old range of building to the southwest marking the site of the original yard. Indeed, if one looks critically at this end of the house, it seems to have the general shape and proportions of an old farmhouse under its facing of shutters and wrought iron fittings. One wonders how it got its name. Was there any connection between the homestead and the twenty shillings that Robert de Olburville had to pay to the king's manor of Winsford? Or with the forestership of his predecessors? Or with subsequent connections with the Royal Forest? Or was it just that a man with the surname of King once lived here? I suppose one can just go on wondering idly for as long as one wants to.

There is a crossing here between the farm and the mill, a line of stepping-stones of a kind through the swift water, but it is one I have never essayed.

The river bends around Kings with a broad sweep, and the mead within its arm is smooth and green. With some fine trees fringing the bank, and patches of wood descending steeply on the other side, the vista here is almost park-like. A little further on a stream breaks down from the east to join the big water, and makes for itself a combe under the shadow of Bradley Ham, the big hill which is a corner-stone to the parish. Partway up the combe is Uppington, another farm.

Uppington is empty at the time of writing, and desolate as such places always are when deserted and unloved. I remember it though, with life and warmth, as when I came to it once in the dusk of an autumn evening, and the lights streamed out from the kitchen windows and the opening door, and there were voices and the flicker of the "telly" from within, and the smell of cooking. It is an ancient farm, for it is "Uppyington" in 1363, and had probably sat where it does for long before that. The house as it stands is a mixture of the old and fairly new. The portion running from north to south obviously represents the older part, which must have faced east into the small narrow yard. The severe-looking main block of today, facing south to a view of the Ham, and overlapping the older fabric at the southwest corner, cannot be so very old, though I don't know when it was built.

The narrow combe which runs back up to Comer's Cross has little fields tucked in under the Ham, pleasantly sunny to face the steep opposing hillside. The Ham itself is a huge chunk of landscape, divided in ownership between three farms – Uppington, Batsham and Bradley –

and until recently had the character of rough moor, mostly of heavy fern, but a few years ago the whole of it, first one part and then another, with the exception of the steepest northern cleaves, was ploughed-out and reseeded. (Of the ploughing-out, and the extreme danger thereof upon the steeper parts, various tales are told, according to which two tractors were lost upon the precipitous shoulder piece, crashing down into the wood below, though luckily without loss of life). In earlier times Bradley Ham was a noted summering-place for cattle. Young Devon bullocks were taken in from all over the district to graze and grow strong there.

Under the shoulder of the Ham is Ham Wood, and between the wood and the river are shelves of level ferny mead. It is a joy to walk here by the river's edge, along the tree-fringed banks at any time, for it is always warm, and sheltered. Only a day or so ago I came this way. "On top" the wind was bitter, cutting like a knife from the north, and the ground hard and set with frost. Dapples of snow lay in nooks and hollows, remainders of the previous days' flurries, and possibly the harbingers of more to come. But here between the wood and the river it was warm, oh so warm. The winter sun, shining from a now-clear pale sky, was drawn and held here as though the land embraced it. The tall old trees of the wood held up their branches to it, and the grass between the fern and rush was already green. The river flowed on in an amber current, broad and deep, with silver-gold ripples, and so clear that one might see every brown stone of its bed. Here was the warmth and shelter of paradise after the biting cold of the hill. Soon I was really hot, and glad to take off my gloves and headscarf. I wished I hadn't got such a heavy coat on. Truly, the warmth was like that of a summer's day. As I stepped along I could not help thinking what might be done with such ground if it were drained. What would it not grow, this alluvial soil in the sun, between the wood and water?

A bit further along I came again to South Hill stepping-stones. Here a fine line of stepping stones march across the river, some twenty-odd big handsome slabs of slate-stone, making a foot passage between Uppington and South Hill. In summer they are easy to pass over, but now, with the water running high and breaking over the tops, I would not care to try. Massive though they are, the river here has a way of shifting things, and so they are clamped now into the riverbed with stakes of iron.

A lane rises from the crossing on the far side, and here is South Hill farm, more usually approached from the Hawkridge road. South Hill is a pleasant place, owing its name to its being on the south side of the hill betwixt itself and Withypool. The old white-washed farmhouse turns its face to the sun across its yard, and attached to the house at one side is an old round-pillared cart linney. This latter is not as fine as the one at

Newland, having only two pillars, but it is good of its kind, and a distinctive bit of local architecture.

The fields of South Hill rise up from the river to the common, and then, a little further onwards to the south, there is upon the hillside a smaller farmstead. This is Blackmoreland. It is an attractive little place, having a south-facing house with a high position and some twenty acres of land. It has of late years been considerably modernised, the old small house being made larger by the conversion and incorporation of the shippon at the east end, and the original yard being laid out as a garden. This latter is charming, its herbaceous beds and grassy patches being intersected by the little splat of fresh water which comes from the spring just above, and which formerly provided refreshment for man and beast alike. Its name may derive from its land being in the beginning black heather ground, or possibly it may be a man's name which is attached. More likely the former, for it is "Blakemore" in 1257.

Below and beyond is Hayes Wood. Hayes is the loveliest bluebell wood I know. Here the oaks grow tall with a fringing of hazel, and in late May or the early days of June the ground beneath becomes a carpet of perfect blue under breaking leaves of green-gold and apple-colour. From the far end there is a path into the wood, and one may walk upon its smooth grass and fill one's eyes with the wonder of all the myriad sapphire heads that crowd together like a reflection of the sky under the leaves of spring. The black rough trunks of the oak trees seem like the columns of some primitive temple, and one walks with reverence. But it is a cheerful wood, with none of the oppression of some.

Here now is Batsham, or to give it its full name, North Batsham. It is a farm of which I have many personal memories, having had great friends here in the past. The farm itself is set halfway up its slope – that is, between river and common – and the house faces south into the yard. Batsham farmhouse is a fine old one, typical of the Exmoor style. Long and low, with a slope-roofed porch and rather shallow silvery slate roof, it is designed to crouch under the weather and give simple solid comfort. Its chimneys rise one each from the gable-ends, and one partway along the ridge – whereabouts I guess the old house originally ended – and its west end butts low into the slope of the ground. There are windows now in the back, giving more light into the interior of the house, but originally there were none, at least on the ground floor, and the place presented the traditional blank walls to the outer world. The walls are rendered all over, and when I first knew the house were cream-coloured, but now they are pink which I do not like so well. In front of the house a small walled patch of front garden intervenes between the main door and the yard.

If one enters the house from the porch, via the main door, one faces the ascending staircase with, on one's right, the big room which must have been the original kitchen, and on one's left the smaller room which would have been the parlour. The big room, which is now the dining room, has a big open fireplace (though a smaller hooded hearth has been inserted within for greater convenience), with a bread oven in the side, and is floored with huge slabs of dark blue slate. These latter my friend always kept polished with wax, and they looked magnificent, like blue-black marble. Further to the right is the present rather small kitchen and beyond that another room, a "back kitchen" until converted to a living room by my friends. Both these last rooms are in the portion of the house beyond the middle chimney, and it is my guess that they were added later. As for the parlour at the other end of the house, still the sitting room, that must represent the very oldest part of the house. My friends, tiring of the modern red-brick fireplace which then graced the room, and finding one day an interlude in the usually ever-pressing needs of farming, took a crowbar and broke it out to see what else was there. Behind it they found an open stone fireplace of the usual kind, spanned by a beam. But above this beam was another bigger and rougher, indicating another even larger fireplace behind. So they set to work to remove the under-beam and supporting walls, trusting to luck that the over-beam with its wider span would hold. It did, and they were able to clear away the debris and see what they had found. Before us – for I was there at the time – yawned the very grandfather of fireplaces. It looked like Stonehenge brought indoors. Huge monolithic slabs of rock set upright shored the sides, the floor – one can barely say hearth – was also of slabs, and the back, made of the roughest walling, had rebated into it a rude point-headed recess. How old it could be, or what the recess might have been, we had no idea. The recess could have been an oven of sorts, but there was no door, and I have never seen an oven in the back of a fireplace, right over the burning hearth, anywhere – it would surely be most inconvenient anyway.

We had a big log fire to celebrate, but alas, the ancient – I almost want to say prehistoric – fireplace, smoked abominably. Nothing anyone could do would make it draw properly, so in the end it had to be walled up again. Whether my friends made any drastic alterations to the primitive fabric in their attempts to make the fire amenable, before they finally blocked it up, I don't know, for I was not there in the final stages. I often wish I had made sketches of it on the spot, for it surely must have been one of the oldest fireplaces on Exmoor, but I omitted to do so, and by the time I got around to calling again it had been walled up once more. I did thereafter make a sketch from memory, which I think is fairly accurate, but that is not quite the same thing as making a record "from life". I have learned since to do things like this when I have the chance, at once, for time and opportunity waits for no man, and so often to delay is to lose.

Upstairs the plan is of the simplest, and one common to most older farmhouses: a passage like a railway corridor running the length of the back of the house, with all bedrooms opening off it frontwards.

How old the house itself, or the main part of it may be, is extremely difficult to judge. Houses of this general pattern were the fashion of the hill-country from Elizabethan times until the middle of the eighteenth century. The change to the four-square type of house did not come until after that, and indeed most of the latter were not built until the nineteenth century. All that can be said here is that the interior woodwork – doors etc. has the look of age about it.

Outside, the buildings that lie mostly to the east side are simple, and have no particular feature. Just across from the house a rill of fresh water falls into a trough with an unceasing rippling sound, and farther back there is a separate garden in the old style.

The site is pleasant, for from the yard one looks straight into the depths of Kings Wood, down to the river, and across to the big sweep of the Ham just opposite. The Ham on this side – its west-facing slope goes with Batsham, and until recently was "rough ground" all overgrown with fern and dotted about with thorn trees. It was very picturesque, but I suppose unprofitable, and so a few years ago its whole sixty acres was broken-out and reseeded. As on the other side of the Ham this reclamation was not accomplished without considerable difficulty, the lower slope being extremely steep and dangerous to work, the job had to be done by "caterpillar", and even that came off its tracks one time. In the end the grass seed had to be "fiddled" in by hand in the old style. To what extent this reclamation has justified itself economically, I don't know, but I notice the gorse and fern persistently trying to come back, and without constant attention the ground would very quickly "go back".

Incidentally, the name Batsham is variously spelt, sometimes being "Batsum" and, more recently, "Batsom". But "Batsham" I feel is more correct, for "ham" is an old English termination whereas the others are not. A curious tale attaches to the name, to wit, that once there were so many bats around about that it was given the name of Bat's Farm.

Southwards from North Batsham there lies an area of enclosed but unattached land known as South Batsham. Now this ground is something of a mystery, for though it is laid out in neat fields, it has neither house nor building upon it, nor has had in any local memory. Yet it is such a definite place, and is entered in the old free suit lists as such, it suits being one. For as long as I have known it, it has gone with South Hill, but once it must have been a separate holding with a homestead. I wandered over it once, trying to locate the possible site of a dwelling place. A bit of a track comes in from the road above, runs down to where several hedges come together, and there stops uncertainly. At this point there is an old water-splat guttered from a spring somewhere, and still obvious. Here I feel must once long ago have been the farmstead. But it must have been very long ago, for there are no obvious remains. Did it perhaps collapse at the time of the Black Death, when so many families died that the agricultural expansion of the thirteenth and fourteenth centuries came to a complete halt and many a new-won holding had to be left to go down again? No-one will ever know.

To return to the river again, as on the winter's day of which I began to speak. Between Batsham and the Bradley Ham ground just under the farm, there is a ford and a footbridge. The narrow bridge, boarded at the sides with tin and closed with gates, is specifically a sheep-bridge, across which the flock may be brought from one side of the river to the other, the ford being much too deep for sheep. From this point one may continue down the river, along the left bank, for there is a hunting path all the way hence to Tarr Steps. The scenery becomes wilder of its kind as the walk continues. The woods begin to close in on either side, Kings Wood, Oakbeer Wood, Pit Wood, Greystone and Well Woods, and then all the thick massed coverts that run almost unbroken right on to Dulverton. These of the aforementioned that are within the parish must have been the principal woods for which there was an appointed woodward in 1257 when the parish of Withypool lay within the Forest – it was his job to see that they were not unlawfully "wasted" or cut down to the detriment of the red deer.

The river winds much on its downward course, looping around the feet of the hills, and alternately the woods crowd right down to the water or give way to patches of mead. The woods are mostly of oaks, tall and ancient, with a fringing of beech, birch and hazel, and by the water alder and sallow. The higher woods are in general open, without undergrowth – the constant grazing of sheep and deer keep them so – and impart a cathedral-like atmosphere, solemn and upward-reaching. Down near the banks though the timber becomes more of a thicket, and often one must pick one's way, with low branches and scratching twigs above and fallen boughs below. Between Oakbeer Wood and Pit Wood however, there occurs a park-like interlude of smooth open slope and grassy mead, beautifully sunny after the enclosing mesh of either. Here the mead has been cleared, drained and reseeded to good effect, and upon it that day grazed a large flock of ewes. That these river meads were valued in olden times for their good grazing one may guess from the fact that both Withypool and Hawkridge seem to have wanted to claim them – upon the old tithe map parts of them are annotated as belonging to Hawkridge – small enclaves of a parish within a parish. The present reclaimed piece is now in Withypool parish but goes with Great Bradley, which farm is in Winsford.

Across the river from here, led by a ford and just visible in its little combe, is Well. It is a sad little place, once a small independent farmstead, but now falling into ruins. Having become unoccupied, some twelve years ago, its lands were divided between two other farms and its house abandoned. It is just one more example of the demise of small farms which is going on all over the country. It lies just outside the parish, on Winsford ground I believe.

The woods close in again now, and the scenery is wholly sylvan, with the river running on, mostly deep, but sometimes breaking on rocks, and singing to itself. Civilisation might be a thousand miles and a thousand years away. That last time that I came this way there suddenly arose before me from the river bank a pair of herons. With their great grey and white arched wings spread against the tarnished gold of the sun-touched woods they flapped their way slowly downstream and out of sight. These noble birds nest somewhere not far off I fancy, though just where I don't know. A little farther on some wild duck took flight from the river with a rush and a quack. Just mallard, but it was nice to see them.

If one keeps one's eyes and ears open, one may also see bigger game. A flick of movement, the crack of a dead stick, and one may see deer going away. What a lovely sight they are! How one's blood kindles at the sight! Creatures of the wild, living without the law, they stir all one's instincts as no bullock or sheep can ever do. Big game in their own right, the quarry of Stone Age hunter, Norman prince and modern rider-to-hounds alike, they are our heritage, one with the heather hills, the tangled combes and the deep oak woods. They belong to Exmoor, and to this our place. How splendid they are, how graceful, how beautiful at all times, even now when their coats are winter-brown and lacking the red-gold of summer. Most splendid of all is the sight of a great stag – and there are some very big stags harbouring in these coverts of the Barle – with his lordly antlers held high in pride.

With reference to antlers, hereabouts are the places to look for them in May, when they are shed from the head and fall amongst the branches and undergrowth. I must confess though that I have never been lucky, for I have never found one yet.

Pit Wood, which is upon one's left hand, is a primaeval sort of place. The hillside is all jagged with outcrops of rock and fallen shattered stones, and many of the trees are fallen too because they are so old. Big bushes of gorse fill the spaces. Half way along the hillside falls back in a sort of hollow with an almost perfect small bowl within it, (is this the origin of the name pit?) and upon the shoulder is a big outcrop of grey rock, a scarp with fallen slabs and boulders at its feet, all in scattered confusion. A knot of tall oak grows from the top, and thick hazel-bushes deck it around. The whole imparts a feeling of druidical significance. Surely rites and mystic ceremonies were once enacted here by the light of the moon? No place was ever more evocative of such things, or more perfectly suited to such. Here if anywhere is the sacred grove of fable – so surely must it have been. But it is imagination only, for there is nothing of either artifice or folk lore here, only a whim of nature.

Onwards a bit further (and through some excruciating mud) and there before one, upon a hillside rising above the woods, one sees Great Bradley, the white walls of farmhouse and farm bungalow coming upon one's vision as a sort of surprise after the archaic atmosphere of the woods. Also the appearance is somewhat confusing to one's sense of orientation, for the farm appears as though to the right hand, whereas one knows it should be to the left. Of course, the answer is that the river bends and loops so much that one is more or less in the state of "looking the wrong way".

Still struggling through the mud, one comes at length to the little stream that comes down from the back of the Ham, and which is the parish boundary. A cart track runs up beside it, going on to Bradley. Bradley itself (properly Great Bradley, for there was once another farm, Little Bradley, close beside it) is just beyond, in Winsford parish, but being within the Withypool postal round has the right to exhibit at the Flower Show, and is thus generally considered to be part of the Withypool community.

Nevertheless it is time to turn back now, and to return to one's centre of life and leave further exploring for another day.

CHAPTER EIGHT

Landacre

Landacre Bridge – here I sit again in the nook of rocks I regard as my very own, just below the bend of the road, and I look once more at the ancient arches, the river, and the hills. Dear Landacre Bridge, how I have loved you ever since I first saw you, many, many years ago. How little has changed in those years, and time is as though it were not.

Here is the grey bridge just before me, its five pointed arches spanning the river with sturdy piers between, and its low parapets rough-textured in the light. Its fabric turns from bright to dark and back again as the sunlight comes and goes and the clouds run scudding on the west wind. Here is the river, broad and strong, running in a steel-blue ribbon from the hills to the bridge, then breaking through the arches in a welter of foam to spread again in a pool of greens and browns and darker depths. I could watch the water for ever in its endless playing of light and colour and sound and movement, ceaseless, never still, yet in its very movement full of a strange harmony that brings peace to oneself.

Beyond are the hills, rough and red with fern, darker towards the heights with heather, and by the river banks are lagoons of tawny rush and sedge. Upstream the river makes a curve around a big bluff, which it has through ages of time sculptured like a cliff, and here are rooted rowans in their proper habitation of rocks. To the right big lines of beech come down the hillside, marking the farthest Landacre enclosures, and a scattering of oak and sallow fringes the river. To the left the road runs on from the bridge-head up over the moor, and there are grassy riding tracks branching off here and there. Before me in the nook by the bridge is a hazel laden with catkins, and across the roadway a silvery rowan growing from the rock, and at my back are the green fields of Landacre. Such is this beloved spot, here on a winter's day.

In the summer, admittedly, the scene is likely to be a little livelier, for many visitors come here now, attracted by the beauty of the spot, and there are many cars parked hereabouts, or along the road, on most days. Folk come to picnic, to splash in the river, to take photos, or just to sit and absorb the lovely unspoilt scenery.

Each according to his taste or means – but I myself prefer it now, in mid-winter, solitary and elemental.

The bridge itself – scheduled as an ancient monument, I believe – is probably of the late fifteenth or early sixteenth century, and must have been first built to carry the packhorse trains that came this way dry-shod over what is in time of spate a deep and dangerous river.[15] The Landacre road was in olden times the main and direct route over the moor from Dunster to North and South Molton, each of these a busy township, and often the strings of packhorses must have come clattering and sliding down the rocky lane from Landacre, over the bridge, and away up the westward rise of the common, splashing hock-deep betimes in the black peaty mud of the track that must have preceded the present metalled surface.

Though the packhorses have long gone, horsemen ride and hooves sound often about the bridge still, for the hounds, both stag and fox, frequent this area, and occasionally meet here, to say nothing of the summer hackers and pony trekkers who come this way. At the time of the autumn drift too, there is much charging to and fro, as the hill ponies are driven up to the pounding-place above, some coming across the bridge, some by way of Sherdon Hutch. There used to be a gate across the lane just above the bridge to stop the ponies (or other beasts) from either going up or coming down the Landacre lane, and it was known as 'the pony gate'.

On the lower side of the bridge there is a pleasant green turfy spot like a lawn, and here on a summer's morning – before the tourists are abroad – I have often sat, right on the rim of the bank, and splashed my feet in the lovely cool water, and marvelled at its clearness, and the glittering of the sun upon its ripples, and been half-intoxicated by its ceaseless singing. From this point one can look upwards at the arches, and admire

[15] According to ENPHER, the bridge is a scheduled ancient monument, probably of late mediaeval origin.

the sound construction of four or five centuries ago which stood up to the raging flood of 1952, when so many other Exmoor bridges went down.

Upon the south-facing hill above the bridge, overlooking the valley and commanding a wide sweep of moorland country, is Landacre itself, the ancient manor. I pass it each time I come to the bridge, and shall pass it again on my way home. It stands nigh the road half-way up the hill, and like all of its kind presents to the beholder a grouping of grey roofs and walls under a knot of beech trees.

Today it stands as a single farm with one attendant cottage of fairly recent erection, but up to about the middle of the nineteenth century there existed here two farms side by side, Higher and Lower Landacre[16]. Upon the tithe map four dwellings are marked, one where the present house stands, one in the middle of the yards (which until recently was still a dwelling), another where is now the bungalow-cottage, and one more upon the roadside where now exists a range of shippons. Presumably these dwellings of 1839 represent the two farmhouses each with an attendant cottage.

Looking back to earliest history, the first mention of Landacre occurs in a Forest Roll of 1257, and then it comes again in 1279 in the document of the second Perambulation of Exmoor Forest, wherein it is described as 'the manor of Landacre' and bidden to be left 'within the Forest'. By the Perambulation of 1298 it was finally put outside the Forest, but right up to the disafforestation of 1815 it continued to have close associations with the latter, and up to the seventeenth century Swainmote courts were still held upon its land. Also it would seem that before the building of Simonsbath House in 1654 the acting forester resided here. At what time Landacre devolved into two separate holdings, and which of the two represented the original settlement, it is impossible to say. The actual sites of the two ancient farmhouses seem to have been, of Lower Landacre, the place between the two yards (until recently still a dwelling and possibly incorporating something of the earlier fabric), which would have faced eastwards across the further yard; and of Higher Landacre, the site of the present bungalow-cottage, which would have faced south into the near yard.

The present house was begun, I believe, about 1760, as the new farmhouse of Lower Landacre, but it was either finished, added-to or extensively repaired after the purchase by the Notleys in 1843 of both farms, and henceforth became the residence of the property. The house as it stands is set on the far side of its yard, facing south out over the valley with a fine view, and is a good four-square example of late Georgian farmhouse building. Within, the rooms are spacious and lofty, con-

[16] The 1904 6″ OS map still shows Higher and Lower Landacre.

trasting much with the low-ceilinged rooms of most of the older Exmoor houses.

With Landacre goes the "freehold" of Withypool Common. The owner of Landacre is still "Lord of the Soil" of all this stretch of wild open moorland, and Landacre in both past and present times must be accounted the most important of the farms of Withypool.

Incidentally, the name seems anciently to have derived from "Long acre" – it is in fact "Longum Acum" in 1257, "Langalere" in 1279, and "Langacre" in 1298, and has always been pronounced "Lanacre". It is hard to understand how the 'd' came in to the spelling.

Down by the river, just above the bridge, are two meadows known as the Court Hams. Here in ancient times were held the Swainmote Courts.

Every year, on the morning after Ascension Day, there assembled here in open-air conclave all those folk of Devon and Somerset who had rights, duties, or any other interests upon the Forest of Exmoor. The chief function of the Swainmote was to settle matters concerning the depasturing or agistment of beasts upon the Forest – for in addition to being a royal hunting ground, the Forest served also as a vast grazing area, it being the custom of the Forest to take in some thousands of sheep, cattle, and horses each summer to eat-off the herbage surplus to requirements of the deer – from which a considerable profit accrued to the Crown.

Foremost at this assembly, after the Forest officials, were the free suitors of Withypool and Hawkridge. These were fifty-two in number, occupiers of the ancient farmsteads of these two parishes, and they held a peculiar position of importance in the affairs of the Forest. They claimed of right certain privileges upon the Forest, but in return were bound to render certain personal services thereto. The rights of the free suitors, similar to those they enjoyed upon their own commons, were free pasturage for sheep, cattle and horses in certain numbers, the right to cut and carry away as much turf, heath and fern as they could themselves consume on their own tenements, and the right to fish in the rivers of the Forest. Also they had exemption from jury service at the assizes, and freedom to buy and sell at the markets without toll. With regard to the number of beasts they might turn into the Forest, these would seem to have been, apiece, 140 sheep (in ancient times for the daylight hours only, the sheep having to be driven out again at nights, but by later times these might lie there altogether), as many cattle as they could overwinter on their own farms, and five horses, mares or colts plus foals. Thus collectively they had rights for 7280 sheep, upwards of 250 horses, and round about 300 to 400 head of cattle. Originally, they had rights for pigs also (apiece, a sow and her piglets, two pigs under two years old and one under three years old), but after the sixteenth century the pasturing of pigs was discontinued – possibly they were too much of a nuisance.

The duties of the free suitors, which they had to perform annually in return for these rights, were to do suit and service at the two Swainmote Courts (at Landacre as aforementioned, and at a secondary court held in Hawkridge churchyard on the morning of the Friday of Pentecost), to 'drive' the Forest on horseback nine times a year upon lawful warning from the forester, to perambulate the Forest bounds once in seven years, and to serve on the jury of the coroner's inquest when any dead body was found within the Forest. The nine drivings of the Forest were five times for horses (three times in summer and twice in winter), three times for cattle (twice before July 25th and once after that if called upon), and once for 'wool' or unshorn sheep (nine days before midsummer).

Next in importance were the suitors-at-large, representatives of those other manors and 'Lordships' surrounding the Forest, who also claimed certain rights within the Forest, but who had to pay for these. Then might come those farmers and landowners from more distant parts who had interest in the agisting of stock, and lastly all those local folk who just wanted to see, listen and talk.

The Swainmote Court held by the river must have been a great gathering of Exmoor folk, and like all such was no doubt an occasion for meeting old friends and acquaintances, exchanging gossip, discussing business, and, of course, eating and drinking. The official business of the day began with a roll-call of the suitors (who had to be there with their 'marks' or branding irons), and anyone of these not present would have a fine attached. Then a jury was empanelled from amongst the free suitors, and the court, presided over by a lawyer appointed by the Warden of the Forest, opened its proceedings. All manner of matters had to be attended to: the presentment of all sorts of petty wrongdoings in the past year, such as trespass, theft, the improper impounding of stock and the general infringement of rules, and fines imposed for these misdemeanours. Then there would be arguments about various rights – as for instance, the persistent but unallowed claim of the farmers of North Molton to free pasturage. Lastly there would be the fixing of the prices for agistment of stock by 'strangers' during the following year. At some time during the day the court adjourned for the free refreshments provided by the Warden. This must have been the highlight of the occasion, and if the weather was fine the assembly would assume the aspect of a grand picnic, but if the weather decided to be bad, then the affair must have been wretched in the extreme, with the wind and rain driving into the meadows and nowhere to find shelter except under a windward bank.

Such was the close connection, of Withypool and Hawkridge in general, and of Landacre in particular, with the Forest of Exmoor in olden times. The Swainmote Courts were held here until the building of Simonsbath House and farm in the heart of the Forest round about 1654, after which the business of the Forest shifted to the latter place. The free suitors, however, continued to ride from Withypool until the final disafforestation of 1815.

If one walks up the hill westwards from Landacre Bridge, one comes at the top to a place where one has a wide view out over what was once the ancient Forest. Here one can sit on a fine day and imagine how this great tract of land once looked, and think a little more about the free suitors.

It is an open breezy spot, and as one sits in the fern just below the road, looking northwards, one can see a long way. Before and below one is the valley of the Barle, with the river shining and winding about the feet of the hills. For up the valley there is to be seen Cow Castle, with its great outcrop of rock, shaped like a pyramid of Egypt, marking the junction of White Water with the Barle. Behind is the long ridge of Winstitchen and somewhere out of sight lies Simonsbath. Beyond that the hills of the high Forest, the sullen Chains, like a roll of cloud on the horizon. To the right is the heathery expanse of Bradymoor, the farther fields of Pickedstones, with the farm just visible on the rim of the hill, and the dark shadow of the fir plantations tumbling down the steep of the hillside to Horsen ford. To the left is the rounded field-chequered hill of Ferny Ball, with its ruined farm in the little combe to the west, and at its foot the stream of Sherdon Water coming to join the river at Sherdon Hutch just down below. West of this rises the big mass of Sherdon Hill, with Lower Sherdon farm set upon it, and Higher Sherdon hidden in a far fold. Farther back one can see Horsen within its windbreak. Nearer, the hedges of Woolcombe Allotment are right beside one, but the farm is out of sight.

Long hedges and boundary-banks pattern the hills, dividing their surface into alternate patches of green grass pasture and rough bleached moor, and the cloud-shadows slide over the contours, moulding them with running darkness and light. The farmsteads catch the sun, and though lonely and remote, yet speak of home. The hand of man is as a cloak upon this archaic land, his touching giving the semblance of humanity. But this patterning is of a brief 150 years only, for prior to about 1820 all the land here before one was an unenclosed untamed wilderness of wild moorland, unaltered since the days of prehistory when the first footsteps of ancient man turned this way to hunt or graze his herds.

Watch the sliding clouds and the wheeling buzzards, and you may see the land as it was long ago and yet not so long ago, one of the three great wildernesses of South-West England: the hills like monstrous billows of the sea, heaving one beyond the other, huge and bare, topped with tawny moor grass and flanked with fern, the valleys soggy with rush-beds, the combes scored to bed-rock, and no trees anywhere larger than the stunted scrub of thorn or sallow down by the waters. No features or landmarks save the form of the hills and the break of the rocks, no roads other than uncertain tracks, and everywhere treacherous bogs waiting to catch the unwary traveller.

Such was the land where the free suitors rode, such a land as one would needs know all one's life to ride, as they did, knowing it from boyhood.

When summoned to drive the Forest, they assembled first at Withypool or Landacre, and then made their start from Wiccombe or Wincombe[17] Head, which is the high ground just above what is now usually called Landacre Brake, upon Bradymoor. Each suitor or his deputy had to turn up mounted on a good horse, and the only valid excuse any of them might give for not being present was "that his wife be in travail with child" or that "they had laid their dough to leaves to be baked that day". (The "warning" for the drive or drift would seem to have been given the night before).

The drive proper began at daybreak, and the time allowed for its completion seems to have been about nine hours, which seems a very short time indeed for the drawing of all this huge area. The ancient Forest itself had an extent of some 22,000 acres, all of it of the wildest nature, and when one considers all the innumerable combes to be combed, the bogs to be circumvented, and the rivers to be forded, one feels the greatest admiration for the fifty-two hard-riding horsemen of Withypool and Hawkridge. There must have been some carefully worked-out teamwork amongst the suitors, else such a drive could never have been successfully accomplished. Their horses too must have been of the toughest to stand up to such a day. One can imagine them coming in to Withypool at last at the end of the day, whooping and holloaing, tired but triumphant, driving the collected beasts – sheep, cattle or ponies as the case might be – down to the pound by the bridge. No cowboys of the Wild West could ever have had a more strenuous ride.

On the occasions when the bounds of Exmoor Forest had to be perambulated, considerable festivity seems to have prevailed, for each of the manors or parishes which abutted upon the Forest had by custom to provide the free suitors with refreshment as they passed along that section. Since no less than thirteen parishes touched upon the bounds, and Exmoor hospitality has never been of the stinted sort, one may fairly

[17] This name is difficult to trace. MacDermot makes no mention of it and local hunting people I asked were not aware of it.

wonder how many of the suitors actually finished the circuit! Upon the ride itself the horsemen are said to have ridden in single file, nose to tail, and upon the actual line of the bounds, regardless of the state of the ground. It was important that the exact boundary-line should be known and remembered.

Again one wonders how it all began – which came first, the farmers or the Forest? Did the suitors give service because their lands were conceded by the Crown, or did they hold their privileges because the Crown had annexed their immemorial grazing-grounds? History gives no answer.

The end of it all came soon after 1815, when an Act was passed for the disafforestation and sale for enclosure of Exmoor Forest. No royal princes had come to hunt within the Forest of Exmoor since the Middle Ages, and for the past century it had been leased to its Wardens, the Aclands, and so outright sale was now deemed more advantageous to the Crown than the continued possession thereof.

Before the final sale the Crown commissioners went very thoroughly into the matter of rights held by custom upon the Forest, and in lieu of the loss of those rights made grants or allotments of Forest land to the various claimants. To the free suitors were made over parcels of land, some thirty-one acres apiece, 1633 acres in all, lying together in a block upon the flank of the Forest closest to Withypool: to wit the land at which one looks gazing westwards towards Sherdon and Sandyway .

On the face of it these allotments might seem a fair enough compensation, but in fact they were not so, as one may see by considering the precise circumstances. Firstly, the awards were made to the owners of the free suit farms, not to the tenants, and consequently the former might do what they liked with the new land and not necessarily grant it to the latter. Secondly, even when an individual farmer managed to get hold of his allotted parcel, thirty-one acres of rough and possibly unfavourably sited moorland was in practice poor exchange for the unlimited roam of 22,000 acres with all the varied seasonal grazing, shelter and water that such a space afforded. And again, there was the matter of fencing, obligatory if he were to maintain his claim to the land, of breaking and seeding the ground if he were to improve it, and possibly legal fees to be incurred in order to substantiate his claim in the first place. All in all, the free suitors came out of the deal very badly, and in the end none of the allotted land seems to have been attached directly to the farms or 'tenements' concerned. Much bitterness was aroused at the time over the matter, and it is only in this last century that it has been entirely forgotten.

After all claims had been met and the various allotments made, the remainder of the ancient Forest was sold, as is well known, to the Knight family, who thereupon set about their great work of reclamation, creating new farms and making roads and long boundary walls across what had hitherto been an unbroken wilderness. Pickedstones and Horsen, and all the farms beyond to the north are their work. Those other farms near to hand, Ferny Ball, Higher and Lower Sherdon, Woolcombe, Sandyway, and some others, are not. Built mostly on land which should have gone to the free suitors, they are the work of other hands, but I do not know their actual history.

So now I come back to sit by the bridge again, and think of many things. One last thing it is fair enough to say of Landacre Bridge: that it, or rather its particular reach, has always been a great place for salmon-poachers. All sorts of tales I have heard, but think they are better unrepeated.

CHAPTER NINE

Pennycombe

Running back from Withypool village away towards the northern hills is one of the prettiest combes I know. Its name is Pennycombe, or more properly Pennycombe Water, for the stream is a strong one, and the combe itself to its main source some five miles long, so it has the right to a dignified appellation.

The best point at which to make, or renew, its acquaintance, is Pennycombe Bridge, just in a dip a few yards along the Exford side road. Here is a pleasant little spot to loiter, as I often do, a little bowl of sunshine on a cold winter's day, sheltered from most of the wind by the encircling hillsides, and with trees and running water to gladden one's heart. The catkins here are always earlier than anywhere else. The little bridge is plain but pleasing, and makes a pretty picture if one sees it from the flanking field. On the one side there are tall fir trees to give a mantling of rich dark green, and through them a glimpse of a steep, rough cleave with a house and terraced garden part-way up the slope. Mill Cleave, both the hillside and the house are called, and the gate of the latter is just here by the bridge. Just here too, another stream, a little rattling one, comes down from a side combe under a thicket of ash and beech to join the Pennycombe Water. On the other side one looks across the meads to the rise of Blackland Ball and the forking of the valley, which occurs about a quarter-mile upwards. As for the road, that goes on up the ridge of the east side of the combe, up a very steep piece of hill known as Spire Rocks – a fair enough indication of the surface of the way before it was metalled.

Pennycombe is a world on its own, in which one could wander for almost a lifetime, and yet feel that one never quite knew it all. At first there is meadow along its banks fairly open, but from the place where it forks – or rather one should say the junction of its waters – it becomes rough and wild in all its parts.

The combe to the left, running up to the north-west, is the shorter, but quite a good scramble. The bottom is narrow and squelchy and tangly, and the hillsides steep and rough, but it is a way I walk often. Here in spring the primroses come early, drawn by the sun that pours on sheltered south-facing lower slopes. The wood that closes in and curves around on the darker side is Blindwell, and under its thicket of hazel and birch there are bluebells in masses in June. In spring also the gorse on the sunnier slopes is a golden glory, and its scent mingles with that of the May bushes in the warmth of the combe. The rounded butt of the hill between the two streams which is Blackland Ball, is a lovely place to sit. The sun shines right upon it, and the great beech hedges which cross it cut off all the cold winds, and one can soak up the sun and listen to the streams, and forget one's cares.

Towards the top of this small combe, where it shallows out to fields again, there arises upon the southern side a knot of big and ancient beeches. So old are they that one has already fallen to lie in a splintering of timber, and some others will not be long going, I fear. Here is the site of Woolpit one of the ancient farms of Withypool, now long gone-down. If one looks about beside and below the trees, one may still discern the remains of walls, low amongst nettles and brambles, and the line of a water-splat is still visible running across the fields from the moor (though it is dry now, the water having been diverted). The site is pleasant and open, with a good laneway leading to or past it – for the Blackland lane runs just by – and one wonders why or when Woolpit went down. No-one seems to remember. On the tithe map it is entered as a living farmstead, and before this, upon the 1809 ordnance map, it is shown marked with the name of 'Whipworthy', though I have never heard it called by that name. In the List of free suitors of 1797 it is 'Woolpitland' and its suit was one. It has been suggested that the title 'Woolpit' may have been derived from some weaving or wool business being carried on from here at some past time – there was a considerable wool trade in North Molton in the eighteenth century.

The stream of the combe, running here between smooth fields, rises about half a mile above, upon the moor beyond the fields, out of Bradymoor Bog. Now between this lesser combe and the larger one, held as between two arms, rises Blackland Hill, a long ridge of high ground running from the Ball right out to the higher moor. It is a hill of note, for it is in the main of reddish sandstone, and its soil of a deeper and better sort than the more general slatey shillity kind.

Two farms sit together on Blackland Hill, Higher and Lower Blackland, and I know them both so well. Of them, and of the higher one in particular, I can write with more knowledge and greater intimacy than of any other, for here I once lived for several years.

Together these two farms may be said to express within themselves all the simple unrecorded history of the Exmoor farms as such. In their setting and in the form and fabric of their buildings, and in their fields small and large, they testify to the nature of the land, and to the pattern of farming that has prevailed for so many centuries, and also to the gradual changes that have come about with the passing years.

One comes to the two farms, if one is approaching by road, along the narrow lane past Woolpit, which dips into the top of the small combe and over the little stream that has sung me home so many times, and then rises to go on the rest of its way between high banks, its way scored deep below the level of the flanking fields. Today it is covered with tarmac, but up to a few years ago its surface was but loose stones and mud, worn to bed-rock in places, and little changed from the days when packhorses clattered and splashed their way along it. In those days five gates spanned its length, each of them opening easily with a wooden horseman's latch, the familiar clack of which I can still remember. So one comes first to Lower Blackland, through whose yard the way runs. To the left is the house and cow-shippon, a pleasing group facing east to the morning sun, and to the right the barn and other buildings set back behind a line of big old beech trees. Often I have sat about here and made sketches of the old buildings, and the beech-trunks molded by the sun and the fine Devon cattle that laze in the meadow beside, but as the upper farm is almost certainly the oldest, it is better for the purpose of this chapter to continue up the lane and begin a general description from there.

Now I write from memory, for at this time of writing I have not been up to the old farm for seven years – when one leaves a place that one loves it is hard to go back, and best not to. Perhaps the place has changed since I knew it, but still I see it in my mind's eye as it was, and so I will describe it.

The lane continues upwards from the lower farm, passing through another gate by which stands a single sentinel beech tree (when I knew it the way underfoot was little more than shelves of bed-rock across which the "splat" ran in two places), and then broadens out and here now is the old farm, shadowed by beech trees and set almost on the crest of the hill. The buildings are grouped to the right, and the octagonal bulk of the round-house, whose walls one sees first, salutes one with something of the look of a castle bastion. To the left the splat of fresh water, guttered down from the moor, falls splashing over a rim of stones, so set to facilitate the filling of a bucket. (This used to be the water supply for the whole farm, man and beast alike). Ahead a gateway leads to Twelve Acres, the biggest field in the parish, and thereabout the lane turns leftwards and becomes a "green" droveway to the moor. So often I have come homewards here, in sunshine with the leaf-patterns dappling the old grey walls, in driving rain with the wet cascading off the eaves and my thoughts turned to hot tea and shelter, in storm, with the boughs of the trees bending and roaring overhead, in fog, in snow, in the moonlight with all things ghostly and mysterious, and upon nights so dark that I could see nothing and judged my whereabouts by the running sound of the splat. Memories! So many of them, some large, some small, some happy and some unhappy, all of them of the sort that bind one to a place. Memories too far beyond my own must cling to it, the memories of seven hundred, perhaps a thousand years, for it was "la Blakelaunde" as long ago as 1270, and it was probably old even then.

Turn to the right, and one is in the yard. Here is the ancient grouping as it has been from earliest times, close and compact, all buildings facing inwards one to another and presenting blank walls to the outer world. So it must have been through the long ages, since first some settler thought the side was good and raised his first roof-tree, for though many times over the walls will have been rebuilt through the centuries, yet the foundations will not have changed, and the yard, worn to bed-rock, is still that same which first knew the hooves of draught oxen and packhorses. It is this close grouping, house, shippons, barn and stable all looking inwards to each other, that proclaims an ancient farm. All the old isolated farmsteads of the hill country followed this pattern, and there is no doubt that it was adhered to from the possible need for defence as well as for the convenience of daily work. In the days before the formation of an organized police force, a man had to protect his home and property against robbers and outlaws himself. Where the plan is departed from it is a sign that either the farm is less ancient or there have been extensive alterations in more recent times.

The house is L-shaped, and the main portion faces south, as is proper – farmhouses were always sited to get the morning sun. Its windows look over a narrow paved walled piece – designed to keep the cattle at a respectful distance – into the yard. As it stands, it is very plain, rough-cast and slate-roofed, but once it was thatched, as were all Exmoor farmhouses and buildings. It was burnt down some time about 100 years ago, and rebuilt in its present form. Within, one may see in the upstairs rooms the line of the old wall-plate which supported the older roof. This must have been much lower than the present one. On looking round one may discern other original features, such as big chimney-breasts which must have once housed open hearths, and the bulge of a bread oven protruding into the cow shippon. In its older form the house must have been of typical long low tall-chimneyed sort, probably of the late sixteenth or early seventeenth century. Just by the back door there is a well, now roofed-over with paving stones and forgotten save for the hollow sound when one treads there. I always thought it a good incentive to murder.

All the other buildings about the yard are of rough weathered grey stone, set in rag or rubble fashion, and are either slated or roofed with tarred "tin". The cow shippon is next to the house, as is the hill-country custom – an echo of the days when man and beast lay together under one roof – and upon the other side the barn, stable, and another shippon are ranged in a long block. The barn is very plain as are all barns in these parts, but within the doorway there is a flooring of big worn timbers – the old 'thresh hold' where in olden times the corn was threshed with flails. A more modern threshing machine, driven by an engine, now fulfils the same function, and continues the tradition of self-sufficiency. The stable and the shippons have lofts or tallets over them for the storage of fodder. When I first knew the place, the shippons all had the traditional ashen stall-trees and cobbled floors, but these have now been replaced by concrete fixtures.

The stable I remember, oh so well, when there were four great draught-horses here within. Blossom, Bonny, Flower, and Princess: two bays, a black and a grey. They were the last to work upon Exmoor. I shut my eyes and I can see them again, in pairs ploughing or drawing the mower, in tandem hauling a heavy load, or three abreast in the binder or with the spring drags. Horses on Blackland Hill! They are gone now, but not forgotten. This last of all the Exmoor teams finally ceased to work in 1962, when my friends, the Misses Common, sold the farm.

In one corner of the yard is a small but interesting building – the ash-house. Here was stored in olden times the rich wood and peat ash from the hearth fires, which in spring was taken out to the fields as an invaluable dressing. The little low-down door through which the ash was drawn is still to be seen.

The splat runs along the lower side of the yard to give easy watering to yarded beasts. This may conclude the survey of the main yard – an ancient self-contained entity. Behind, however, lies another yard, probably added more recently, and having about it ranges of shippons and calf-boxes.

Of the buildings of this second yard, the range on the north side draws attention by its much bolder redder stonework, which contrasts very much with the thin slatey ragwork of the opposite range. This bolder stone, pinkish red or deeper plum-colour, is the red sandstone of the hill that is got by quarrying (the pits from whence it came can still be seen in the fields), whilst the thin grey shale is of the surface stratum, such as lies loosely or breaks in outcrops on the north side of the ridge. Incidentally, this particular range has an external flight of stone steps leading up to the tallet above, so properly justifying the word. (For the term "tallet", though in general use for any loft, is more specifically applied to one having such steps). Hired hands probably slept up here in olden times.

The round house which stands just outside the main yard is interesting. It is one of the few to survive, though most of the bigger farms had such in past times (there was one at Newland, I believe), and its purpose was to house the horse-driven machinery which motivated the thresher within the barn. On days when corn was to be threshed, the horse or horses walked round endlessly within the space of the round house attached to the tackle and so providing, literally, the necessary horse-power.

Behind the farm is the sheep-dip, on the south side the hay barn, with beyond this the sunny little garden piece, and on the other side of the lane-way the ricksplat where the round corn-ricks stand after harvest. Around lie the other little plats that are so useful at lambing-time.

So here one sees a farm which is truly an entity in itself, self-contained, self-sufficient, grown from the soil as much as any tree, and with provision for all needs. Every building, every feature tells some part of its story. Its double yards and plentiful buildings speak of a large holding of land, and indeed it is, or was as I knew it, with its 300 acres, the largest farm in the parish. It was, so I am told, noted as a bullock-farm in olden times, one of the best on Exmoor.

Beyond and around are the fields, reaching for more than a mile from the junction of Pennycombe out to Bradymoor Gate. They too tell a story: the smaller and irregular ones being the oldest and the bigger rectangular ones the more recent. Also, the oldest have the more personal and interesting names, whilst the newer tend to have simple descriptions such as Four Acres, Nine Acres, etc. Curiously, a number of the fields lie over in Exford parish. These seem to have been enclosed from land awarded to the Blackland farms upon the enclosure of Exford South Common in 1851. This awarding of common land to a farm or farms in another parish is unusual, and indicates some peculiar claim. Higher

Blackland farm itself lies right up against the parish boundary, the said boundary running along the line of the hedge immediately above the house and yards, so that in earlier times the open moor must have lapped right up to the homestead. The inference is that the farm itself is much older than the accepted parish bounds, and that anciently its holders claimed grazing rights on both sides. The outlying forty acres by Bradymoor Gate is wholly in Exford parish; and is known as Blackland Allotments.

The 'Blackland' speaks of a heather hill, for the term 'black' in Exmoor etymology means heather – though sometimes peat also – and if you wonder why, look at an expanse of heather on a wet winter's day. Once, when the first settlers came, the ridge between the two arms of the Pennycombe Water must have been dark with thick black heather.

Now one may look again at Lower Blackland. At some time in past history this second farm was carved out just beside the older one. The arrangement, that of two farms side by side, or one above the other, is common in the West Country generally. The prefixes Higher and Lower, East and West, North and South, Great or Little, litter the maps of this region. How this arrangement came about one can only guess, but the guess is that when a farming family divided up – as perhaps in the instance of two brothers married and with families – an effort was made to establish another homestead, giving to it some of the land already taken-in and adding a bit more by fresh enclosure. (Some of the Blackland fields seem to have belonged first to one farm and then to the other in past times).

Lower Blackland has from its looser grouping the aspect of a less ancient farm, but it is old enough anyway. The house, which faces east, shows the big bulge of a bread-oven on its face and has a deep recessed porch to its main door, to which one comes over a wide expanse of cobbling. I am told that there is a stone somewhere in the fabric with the date "16" upon it, though I have not seen it myself. The cow shippon is of one block with the house, at the south end, and its door opens on to the same cobbles whereby one approaches the house door, so that here one sees even more clearly the ancient connection. Once the whole range was thatched, but the thatch has long gone in favour of slate and "tin".

The barn and other buildings opposite are very plain, and not extensive in comparison with those of the higher farm.

As I have said, I like to linger here and make sketches. The house is cream-washed, and there is a neat little flower garden along part of the front, and behind are tall trees. There are – or used to be – handsome Muscovy ducks strutting around who, upon the slightest pretext, would take off and plane down the slope with a great showing of black-and-white wings. The place has a feeling of peace and contentment, and even the cattle seem to want to laze when they come into the yard-space. Of the barn beyond though, I have memories of busier days, those of the long strenuous hours of shearing at midsummer time.

I could go on for long remembering and recalling so much about these two farms, both so well-known and loved, but they must be left for now. So my footsteps must turn in fact or memory up over the ridge of the hill, across Blackland fields, and into the main branch of Pennycombe.

In passing over one may note the gutter-lines that rim the ball contour-wise. Once they channelled water from the springs to the hillside, and when breached in the spring, irrigated the steep sunny slopes so that a flush of grass came early. These carefully engineered gutters are to be seen upon many Exmoor hillsides, and their invention is credited to the Quartleys of Molland, those pioneering agriculturists of the eighteenth century. (Billingsley noted this method of irrigation upon his tour at the end of that century, and said of it that by its means one might have grass fit for ewes by Candlemas). Also there are on both sides of the hill outlying linhays, where beasts could be out-wintered and fed away from the main yards, but these are unused and falling down now.

Pennycombe is, as I have said, a world in itself. Once down in its depths by the rushing stream one is, or seems, far from everything else. By the stream there are alternately grassy meads and rushy patches, and the steep hillsides that close in are a tangle of wood and brake, broken in places by outcrops of rocks. I love to walk here in spring, when the primroses are out, and the fern is down so that I can pick my way more easily on the rougher parts, and the hills cut off the cold spring winds. One can work one's way right up to Chibbet Ford if one knows the ground.

Once though, the combe was not so peaceful. There was for a while in the nineteenth century, a small iron-mine in the hills under Blackland. That part of the narrow valley is still known as "Mining Cleave" and one can still find the entrances to the levels if one knows where to look. Also one can trace the ramp of the "tramway" up the opposing hillside, whence the ore was drawn to the top by a trolley system. This mining venture however did not prove economic, and the mine closed down. For this I confess to feeling thankful, for Pennycombe in its natural state is such a wild pretty valley, and I prefer it to remain so, with only the cry of the hounds in winter and the song of the birds in summer to break its quiet.

Upon the hill north-east above Pennycombe stands Halsgrove, another farm of the parish. It is a place of moderate size, with the house standing somewhat aside from the yard, showing a less ancient date than those previously described. The farm itself is ancient though, being

'Haselgrove' in 1333. There used to be rough-pillared standings in the old yard, I remember, but there has been much modernization here of recent years, and I do not know if any of the old fabric is left.

Halsgrove is remembered locally for its slighting of Sally the witch. Sally Pippen was a little old woman who lived in a little bit of a cottage higher up Pennycombe, up above the rocks. She lived, as others of her kind have done, on bits-and-scraps, and often went gathering shreds of wool which she might, when she had got a bundle, sell for a few pence. Reputedly, she was a witch, and most people treated her with respect. One day she came to Halsgrove and asked the farmer if he had any wool she might pick. He, being in a bad mood, answered her roughly and said he had no wool on the place. "Ah, but 'ee will have by morning," said Sally. And in the morning he found a score of his very best sheep dead of some mysterious complaint. No-one had any doubts but that Sally had cast a spell on them. How long ago this was, no-one remembers, and Sally's little hut has long fallen down, though its foundations may still be discovered by those who know where to look. The rough cleave to the north east of Higher Blackland is still known as "Sallys" in memory of her.

Now, if having explored Pennycombe proper, one goes back to the bridge whence one started and follows up the tiny stream that comes from the side-combe there, one will come to two more farms, the last of this parish to be described. They sit one each side of the combe near its top, and one lane serves them both. The first is Foxtwitchen, itself now divided into two separate holdings, and the other is Weatherslade. The first farm, the 'Foxtwichene' of 1270, crouches low against the wind on its rim of hill, and has house, barn and shippons looking inwards to a sloping yard in the old style. It is a pleasant, sunny place, with whitewashed house, and used to have some big trees around, though these have now been felled. Since, however, being parted from the bulk of its land – it now has only a few acres – it has reverted to its secondary local name, that of Ley, and is so known, the primary name being now attached to the modern house that stands above. The present Foxtwitchen is a large residence built within the century, close by and upon the land of the old farm. The name is interesting. The component 'twitchen' – not infrequent in the Exmoor country – comes from the old English 'twicene', meaning crossways. The prefix 'Fox' seems plain enough (there are always foxes in the combe below), but what cross or divergence of ways there might have been here in olden times is not at all clear.

Across the combe upon the rise is Weatherslade, and once again here is a farm of which I have many memories. If one comes to it by way of the lane, one sees from the dip of the combe its buildings blank-walled and buttressed on the rise above, and here again is that semblance of a fortress which one feels on approaching so many of the ancient hill-farms. The lane twists and rises, and here now is the old yard upon one's right, with the house and some more buildings just beyond. The present house, detached from the older buildings and facing across the fields to a wider view, is of fairly recent construction. The old house stood with the grey buildings of the yard, facing into the yard – in this case looking westwards – and its remains can still be discerned, doing duty now as shippon and tallet.

How well I remember the yard full of ponies at the end of each October! For the owner, Mr F. Milton, is a great breeder of Exmoor ponies, and here they come in clattering herd each autumn for the sorting and branding. I remember the cattle too, red Devons who mill about the yard and fill the shippons in winter. I remember the packing of hay and oaten sheaves into the tallets in the summer days, and most of all perhaps, I remember that winter when the snow was up to the bellies of the beasts and the roofs bore up the weight of nearly three feet of snow.

The fields of the farm run up to Room Hill, 1200 feet at the top, and here are Devon cattle and Closewool sheep, and in summer corn as well. Weatherslade is the last of the Withypool farms to grow corn. Once corn was grown on every farm, oats for the stock and wheat for bread, and some barley as well, but year by year the acreage has declined – without hand-labour any grain-crop is difficult to harvest in this country of high rainfall – and now only upon Weatherslade do oats still raise their frothy golden heads in late summer.

Many tales I have heard told of Weatherslade, but the most interesting is that of the cats of Room Hill. Once, it seems, there lived upon the far side of Room Hill, amongst the rocks and scrub, a remarkable race of fierce wild cats. They existed there until the early years of the twentieth century, and in hard winters they would come up and prowl about the Weatherslade fields. According to Mr Milton, who remembers seeing the last of them occasionally in his boyhood, they were larger than any ordinary domestic cats, and striped sandy-grey in colour, thick-tailed, long legged, and moved with a peculiar slinking gait. In nature they were savage, and the farm-cats were afraid of them, and no dog would tackle any of them. Now, "wild cats" – that is, domestic cats gone feral – are, or used to be, very common in the West Country, but from the vivid and detailed description given me by Mr Milton, I have no doubt at all in my own mind that these cats of Room Hill were no feral pussies, but true wild cats, a last remnant of *Felis silvestris*, the British Wild Cat, surviving remarkably in this remote corner of moorland long after their extinction in the rest of southern England. That they were finally killed-out – round about the time of the 1920s, I suppose – is in many ways to be regretted, though this was, I suppose inevitable in a sheep-country.

As to the name "Weatherslade" I am not sure if the prefix derives from "weather" or "wether", but "slade" is a term in these parts meaning shallow slope or valley of that nature.

Now the tally of the ancient farms of Withypool is with this chapter complete.

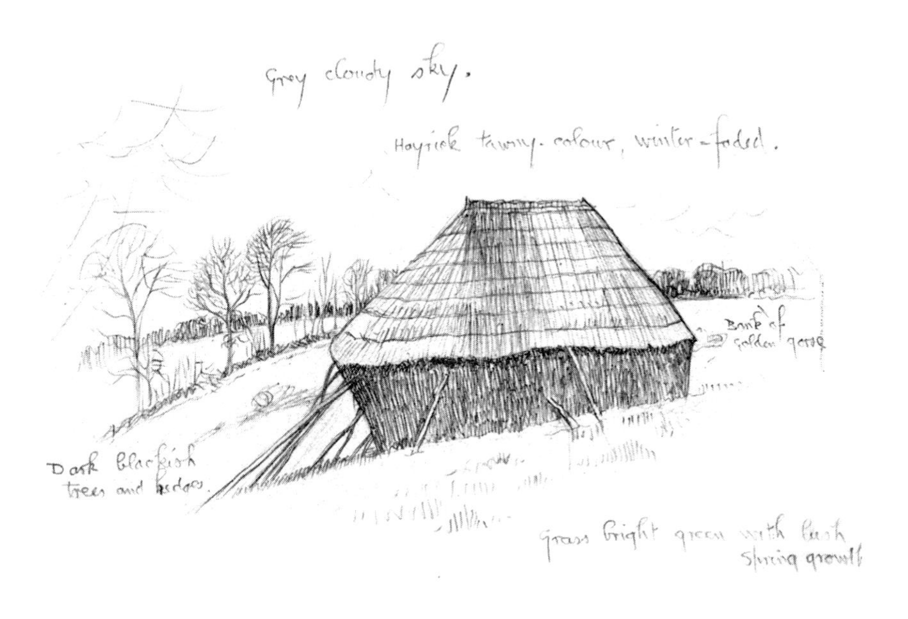

CHAPTER TEN

By Kitridge Lane to Bradymoor

Up Kitridge Lane to Bradymoor is one of my favourite walks. So once again I will set off past the church, past the pretty garden patch, round the corner by the Royal Oak, past the sad little empty house known as Raymond's, and up by the fork where a signpost says "Unfit for Motors".

Just as one rounds the corner one sees to the left hand a cottage and garden, which I think the prettiest in Withypool. Its name is Oliver's Cottage. The small house, set just a few paces back from the road, is slate-roofed and cream-washed and has big chimneys at either end which give it character and dignity. A front door between four small windows looks straight at one, and the door itself, of the old 'stable' type, is ever-welcoming when its top is open to the sunshine on a bright morning. The paintwork is of light blue, a turquoise shade, and over the face of the house is a climbing rose and a japonica. The tiny front garden that fills the space between house and road, now dappled with snowdrops, is in the summer like a box full of flowers. Against one window there is a bay tree, well rooted in the ground and flourishing exceedingly, showing that even Mediterranean plants will settle in the hill country if you make them happy, and in the far corner of the plot arises a dark yew which makes a sober foil for all the gayer colour. As one continues round the corner, one sees over a side-gate the back of the cottage with its roof sweeping right down like a brim to its back door, and has a glimpse of the big garden that sweeps upwards vista-like to a background of fine trees. "Ditched" walls, stone steps, a lawn, and many flower-beds, all from spring to autumn filled with lovely flowers of every sort – I always linger as I pass this way, for cottage and garden together with the rim of the moor beyond make a perfect picture.

Once round the corner one takes the left-hand lane at the aforesaid fork and starts to ascend to rising ground. On the left there is the upper gate to the Rectory, and the driveway to a larger house, its banks carpeted at the moment with snowdrops and spring heath – I linger here too, for I always make the most of other people's gardens – and then a little further on to the right, the white walls of the cottage called Dadhays appear beyond a fringe of poplar saplings.

Dadhays is an interesting little place. The house is set facing the land, right upon it, with a slope-roofed porch shading the door, and behind the house is a yard-space where may be discerned some pillared out-buildings. The dwelling as it stands today is slate-roofed, but up to a few years ago it was thatched in the old style. It was the last of the dwellings of Withypool to retain its thatch, and now this too is gone, and there no longer is any thatched roof in the parish at all. Very pretty it used to look in those former times, with its roof like a bonnet and its climbing roses touching the low eaves. In those times too the single storey part extending to the north-west was a small barn, but is now an extension to the dwelling. As the ground drops away sharply at the back, there are or were small standings beneath the house itself as well. From all of which it can be seen that Dadhays was once a small farmstead. It was indeed one of the ancient holdings of Withypool, entered on the free suit lists with a suit of one. Until recently, when it was amalgamated with a larger farm (Halsgrove) it had some twenty acres of its own. As an ancient holding though it poses some questions. The site is northerly, the land falling away steeply to the north, and the house perforce set to the south of its very narrow yard, and facing outwards. It is not a desirable site, and not such as was usually taken by early settlers. However, "there it be".

A former owner loved it very much, and planted many flowers around it. Once there were gentians, peacock-blue, in the narrow raised border before the little house, and daffodils and narcissus of the rarer sorts, and small alpine treasures. (How often I have lingered here – whoever plants flowers upon the wayside, or a garden where passers-by can see it, does a great public service, and is a public benefactor most truly). The gentians and the rarer plants have now gone, but the hardier ones, snowdrops, crocus and daffodils, still come along the banks to salute the spring, and nod under the shimmering poplar saplings that arise nearby. Most of all though, I always notice and remember the many brave bold deep-yellow daffodils of the old-fashioned double sort that come early here, and are like golden sunbursts on blustery April days.

The lane goes on, between high banks, and then begins the rise of Kitridge proper up to the top of the hill. There are field gateways at intervals here and there, which are as windows in a corridor, giving views out over the countryside, and at each one I like to stop for a few moments. Below on the right is Pennycombe, deep and tangly, with the sound of its waters coming up to meet one. Here at one gate is the top of Blindwell or "Sloley's Wood" as we more commonly know it, a thicket of hazel, birch, and thorn, and deep fern. At the moment its fringe, which is all of hazel, is yellow with hanging catkins, whilst the birch trees below lift up heads of swelling purple-crimson buds. Later there will be primroses and bluebells in masses.

The lane itself is full of interest at all seasons. In spring there are golden saxifrages, delicate white wood-sorrels, big heath violets, pennyworts, polished celandines, and of course dear shaggy dandelions as big as possible. (How I love dandelions – why does everyone despise them? They are amongst the most joyous of flowers). In summer the banks are thick with ferns and tall with foxgloves, and full of red campions and yellow hawkweeds. Towards autumn the sky blue sheep's-bit opens like eyes amongst the shining grasses, and the banks beneath the woody hedge-stock sprouts fungi of many sorts. Brambles and wild raspberries hang down with an abundance of fruit, and render one's walk slower than ever. Even in winter one may find mosses and lichens and ivy leaves of many forms, and pluck deep dusky purple bramble leaves.

As the lane rises up the steep, its big hedges arch over and meet together, making it a sylvan tunnel, and by the road-edge runs a tiny stream, a spring that comes from somewhere and goes to nowhere along its rocky gutter. The arching branches are bare now, but in May when all the beech leaves break forth in fluttering glory this stretch of lane becomes a veritable corridor of fairyland. Later, when the autumn leaves begin to fall, there is always a rich harvest of 'leaf-mould' to be gathered here, for the red leaves blow and funnel-up in big drifts, and often I have trundled a barrow or carried a sack up the steep to go home laden with the rich spoil for my garden.

There are always wrens in the hedges here. I hear their little song, and see them flit like small brown leaves upon the wind. Once I saw five come out of a hole under a mossy root, one after the other. Mother, father, and the family, I suppose – I believe wrens are family-conscious.

Sometimes a small lizard will dart across the road, though not very often, for they are rare. Slow-worms are commoner. Hedgehogs are also fairly common – alas, I almost always see them squashed, run over by cars. (I wonder why they always seem to be abroad in the roads at night?) Sometimes one sees foxes – on one occasion a big old dog-fox came out of a gateway and walked coolly up the road a few yards ahead of me for quite a way up the lane, quite unconcerned, before turning off over a bank. With Blindwell on one side and Newland Wood on the other, both of which have earths, there are often foxes about.

At the top of the hill the land widens out, and the sun comes in, and one emerges into the light with a sense of having arrived somewhere. Here the hedges are cut back and there are wide views all around. Always I stop at my favourite gate under the tree on the right-hand side and look across to Blackland Hill with its two farms upon the top, and farther off to the rim of Dunkery and the rise of Alderman's Barrow upon the skyline. On the other side of the road is the field known as Great Kitridge, right on the top of the hill, and one of the largest in the parish, and hence one looks to all the sweeping moor beyond the Barle. Once kites must have soared and roosted here, for Kitridge means 'Kite Ridge' – the component occurs in several other Exmoor place-names.

A little further along, the farm lanes to Blackland and to Hillway branch off right and left, and then the road goes on with grassy verges and under some big trees until a gate abruptly bars the way. Here is the end of the tarmac, and of Kitridge Lane, and here begins the moor.

Through the gate, and one is upon Bradymoor, that expanse of heathery moor which though part of Withypool Common yet has an entity of its own. That portion upon which the lane debouches is a long strip, with a hedge on one side and a wall on the other, reminiscent of a broad drove-road, and it is here that the ponies are gathered every October at the autumn drift. But to go on – only the roughest of tracks now proceeds, just a muddy way of ruts and rushes, though once it was the old riding-road to Simonsbath. One crosses the small rill of fresh water that comes from Bradymoor Bog and is guttered down to Hillway, and goes on to cross over the Exford-Landacre road. The wall on the right falls away to open moor, and half-a-mile further on the last of the Landacre enclosures also drop away to the left, along the combe known now as Landacre Brake – though anciently as Wincombe. (This is the point from which the free suitors started their ride when they drove the Forest in ancient times). Here is another of my favourite sitting-places, always sheltered, and with a pleasing view across to Brightworthy, and Dillacombe. Before it was burnt out a few years ago it was a thicket of gorse, the sight and scent of which in May-time was truly glorious. Hence now is high heather moor, with the wet splashy, rutty, peaty, and in places washed-out track running on between the tussocks, and just the sky overhead, and the small moor-birds rising all round. As one goes along, picking one's way from one bit of squelching track to another, one has some idea of what travel was like in these parts before the making of roads (though to be fair, the ways, when horsemen only passed along them, were probably not at all as bad as they are now with tractors and Land Rovers chewing them up). Upon the middle of the moor there rises a spring, which breaks in three small heads, and the track passes just beneath, so that the three rills run together upon it, and then pour away in a tunnel-like score under the heather. To sit here in the sun on a hot summer's day with the scent of the heather closing upon one, and to drink the sweet water and press one's hands upon the damp sphagnum moss, is bliss. This favourite nameless spot I call "the Fairy Springs" for I am sure naiads ought to play here on moonlit nights.

After this the ground becomes more ferny, and amongst the fern there are embedded numerous big white stones of marble-rock. They seem to be of natural origin, cast about by some whim of Nature, and in no wise the handiwork of man. However they make good rubbing posts for the moor sheep. Beyond these a hedge appears, and here again is the parish and Forest boundary. The hill here must be Clampard's Ball, so called in old Forest documents, though I have never heard it spoken-of as such. A gate in the hedge gives access to the continuance of the track under Pickedstones to Horsen Ford and Cow Castle, a fine walk, but if one would for the scope of this small book keep with the bounds of Withypool, one must now turn back.

Returning, one may think of various things, and also probably see the ponies, if one has not already done so.

Bradymoor, as I have said, is good heather moor, or was. But here, as with other parts of the common, there has been a deterioration of the heather in the past twenty years. To me, knowing Bradymoor very intimately, it is most marked. The heather here used to be amongst the most glorious on all Exmoor, in late summer a purple cloak across this part of the common, almost intoxicating in its scent and colour, and in spring full of green-brown resurgent life. Now its extent is less, the bracken, dwarf-gorse and moor-grass tending to take its place, and its vigour is also less, the flower being poorer and the spring growth often shrivelled-looking. Whether some disease ails it, or whether its decline is due just to the reasons already given for the same upon the common as a whole, I do not know.

Two other things I often notice hereabouts: the presence of low banks that run here and there under the heather, and the peculiar ridge-formation of the ground in places. The former can only be the remains of old, or attempted, field-banks, and show that once upon a time someone must have tried to take in parts of the moor. How long ago, though, no-one can say. In the early years of the nineteenth century the then occupant of Landacre enclosed an amount of ground on the south-west side to make additional fields for that farm (with or without manorial permission), but these old sunken broken bank-lines give one the impression of being very much older than this. Perhaps they are the work of that John of Landacre who sought unlawfully to enclose ground hereabouts in the thirteenth century at a time when this land – Bradymoor – was considered to be within the Forest, and who was subsequently forced to relinquish the ground.

The second peculiarity, less obvious, and probably only noticeable to one who habitually walks the moor, often traversing its rough ground away from the existing tracks, is the presence of a ridge-and-furrow formation in certain places. Now this ridge-formation is present on some parts of the common as well, though only noticeable under certain weather conditions, those conditions being melting snow or the low light of the setting sun at certain times of the year. It is most marked by the former, the snow lying for a fraction longer in the slight and ordinarily unnoticeable hollows than upon the ridging. I remember after one bout of snow looking across from Bradymoor to the common beyond Landacre Bridge, and seeing with some surprise that all of the bluff of land between the bridge and Sherdon Hutch, and also a part of Brightworthy Hill, was strip-lined in this fashion, marked-out visually by thin lines of melting snow. I have also noticed the same peculiarity on the western hill above Knighton Combe, nearer to Withypool.

This curious patterning, which runs always up-and-down the slopes, never contour-wise, and which consists of long narrow strips which I compute to be about six feet wide from furrow to furrow, must certainly be the marks of ancient ploughing. But by whom, and how long ago? It is known that commoners might of old cultivate a small temporary patch of corn on the Hill in times of great need, but this strip-marking is something quite different to the ordinary small-field ploughing of the hill-country. To my mind it denotes the work, of the old mediaeval, or Saxon, long-team ox-plough, and seems to indicate that once, long, long ago, some concerted effort was made to break the moor hereabouts. All of which is alien to the ordinary pattern of individual hill-country settlement, and brings one back to the original and uncertain origin of Withypool. All that I can say further is that, with one exception in a certain part of Hawkridge, I have never seen this strip-patterning anywhere else on Exmoor.

Now here are the ponies, grazing amongst the heather, picking for such shoots, tips, and blades as they may find, and probably mosses and lichens as well. How they seem one with the moor, wild creatures in a wild land; their winter coats blending in deep harmony with the colours of the moor so that one hardly sees them unless they are upon the skyline. Bay and brown, black points and mealy underparts, all matching perfectly with red fern and winter heather and the sere moor-grass. They seem autochthons, born of the earth, not beasts of man as are the sheep and cattle, and belong with the buzzards, the foxes and the deer. I walk towards them, looking for their brands and tail-nicks, and they raise their heads, and their mealy noses shine flour-white. For a moment they look at me, allowing me to come to about fifty yards distance, and then they wheel and gallop away, their small hard hooves drumming on the moor, and then they are gone, vanished like ghosts.

They are true Exmoor ponies, the small remainder of what was once the big Withypool Hill herd, the best moor-bred herd in the country. Once there were hundreds of them, now there are little more than a score. Yet still they keep their identity, and do not fraternize with the other mixed herd that runs on the other side of the Hill. They stay mostly upon Bradymoor, seeming to prefer it to the other parts of the common, probably because it is sunny-sloped and sheltered from the winter winds.

Of Exmoor ponies in general, their history, conformation and virtues, I have already written much in two preceding books, but nevertheless it is fitting that I say here what I know of them upon the Hill, for no account of Withypool would be complete without some description of these remarkable little horses.

From time immemorial the ponies have been here upon the Hill. Though nominally owned by the farmers who have common rights, they live all the year round upon the Hill, and remain in all their ways truly creatures of the wild. Their colouring is that of wild animals, and their size and general conformation agrees with what is known of the original wild horses of prehistory. Their hardiness and toughness is unparalleled. I myself have no doubt that they are directly descended from the prehistoric wild horses of Western Europe, and represent a remarkable survival into modern times of the little native wild horses of the region.[18]

With regard to the more recent history of the ponies, one main line of ancestry goes back to the ancient Exmoor Forest herd. Until the disafforestation of 1815 there ran upon the Forest a remarkable herd of ponies, numbering more than 400 – possibly nearer 1000 – who were virtually wild creatures living upon a land that was higher and harsher than even Withypool Hill. Billingsley, the agricultural commentator who passed over the forest in 1798, noticed these ponies and the severe conditions

[18] The debate over the origin of the ponies continues. See Sue Baker's *Survival of the Fittest: A Natural History of the Exmoor Pony*, (1993) and later work by vet Peter Green *The free-living ponies within the Exmoor National Park: Their Status, welfare and future*, (2013).

under which they lived, and stated that they never left the Forest. Upon the disafforestation the ponies were driven down off the Forest, and the last Warden, Sir Thomas Acland, took 400 of them to Old Ashway, from where they went to Winsford Hill as the Acland herd. The remainder were sold to various buyers, one of whom was a Mr Milton of Withypool. So a contingent of these ponies was brought to run on Withypool Hill, and the descendants thereof are still here.

It has been argued that since for many centuries it was the custom for holders of 'rights' to turn out upon both common and Forest, horses of any sort, the Exmoor Pony cannot be regarded as an unmixed aboriginal breed. However, to anyone with a knowledge of the moor and the ponies, this is not borne out. Firstly, the stock turned out in olden times would itself be mainly of the same local indigenous sort – the Exmoor being the 'horse of the country' – and secondly, under the harsh natural conditions of life on the high moor, cross-bred stock would not survive for long unfed and untended by man. Nature is a great selector. Only the true native pony can endure the long hard winter of the open moor. This is something which breeders know, that any sort of cross-breeding reduces the innate hardiness of the natural Exmoor.

The cycle of life for the ponies of the Hill begins about May, when most of the foals are born (though some are born earlier, and a few later). The wild colouring is even more marked in the young, the mealy underparts, muzzles and eye-cingles being strongly accentuated. Through the lazy summer months the youngsters graze with their mothers in the family herd, presided over by the ruling stallion who keeps the herd together – and also intruders away. Then October comes, and with it the annual pony gathering or 'drift'. This usually takes place on the last Saturday before Bampton Fair, which is on the last Thursday of the month. I remember the drifts of past years, when there were many ponies on the Hill, not the few that there are now, most farmers in the parish then possessing a considerable number. All the owners concerned, together with as many friends as possible, assembled upon horseback early in the morning, usually at Withypool, and set out to 'drive the Hill' to gather up the ponies. The plan of campaign was always to drive the ponies who might be on the main part of the common down to Sherdon Hutch, push them through the ford there, and then run them up across Bradymoor to the narrow neck of moor adjacent to Kitridge lane, where they were held as in a pound. The last moments of the drift, when the concerted herd of some hundred or so ponies came thundering up the final stretch, driven hard by holloaing whip-cracking outriders, was always wildly exciting, and as fine a spectacle as any Wild West film could show. Once in the improvised pound, the herd was held by the riders forming a rank along the open moor end, so preventing any of the ponies breaking-back.

The remainder of the day was spent sorting the ponies. The owners moved amongst the wild-eyed milling creatures, studying the brands, and one by one turning them, each mare with her foal, through one or other of the gates into lane or field, until each of the individual herds was complete, and might be driven off by its owner. At the end of the day all the ponies were off the Hill, and the many hoofs went rattling down the lanes of the parish to the various farms.

The following Monday was branding-day, when the youngsters were caught-out in the home yards and branded. So much excitement! The ponies plunging and wheeling in yard and shippon, the branding irons put in the kitchen fire, the arrival of the officials of the Exmoor Pony Society, and also prospective private purchasers, the catching-out of the lusty foals (incidentally the word 'foal' was never used, only 'colt', sex being defined by the terms 'horse colt' or 'mare colt') and the final selection of those to be sold and those to be returned to the Hill.

The next day or thereabout the stock to be retained went back to the Hill again. Then on the Thursday the surplus youngsters, those not privately sold, were boxed for Bampton Fair. (Once the ponies were driven all the way along the road, but that was before my time). Bampton Fair was a spectacle all in itself, with ponies from all over Exmoor penned in their hundreds, but one for which I never had much taste. The sight of the poor little wild things crammed into pens, terrified and awaiting an unknown fate, is something I hate to see. Much rather would I see and remember them upon their native moor.

So was the great annual drift, and so it still is, excepting that the numbers have dwindled now, and the gathering presents so much less of a spectacle. Why this is so I do not really know, for good Exmoors bring good prices today, but seemingly few of the commoners want to bother, and those folk who go in for professional showing seem to prefer to keep their show stock in-ground. (But a propos of the latter, it is upon the moor that the best and toughest stock is bred – the moor and the ponies belong together).

After the gathering, and the return to the Hill, the moor is sorrowful for a while with the calling of the mares for their lost children, but after a time they forget, and as for each another foal grows inside them Nature gives them content.

Then comes winter, long, hard and relentless. Somehow the ponies survive. Occasionally, in times of great severity, attempts have been made to give them hay, but always these humane efforts have proved to be misguided. In the first place, since it is impossible in deep snow to take the fodder to where the ponies lie, they must perforce be tempted out from their chosen places of shelter in the bitter wind, and secondly, they are for the most part contemptuous of hay anyway, and often will not touch it. Left to themselves, they will always draw down into a shelter, and delve in the snow for a picking of some herbaceous stuff or other, and so survive.

I remember 1963. The preceding autumn Mr Fred Milton had turned some twenty ponies back on the moor, and these, together with a few belonging to another owner, made up a small compact herd. After the snow set in on Boxing Day, the ponies were not seen again, with but one exception, until the following March. The one instance was when Landacre Farm sent word – just before the wires came down – that the herd had got over the styles into the Landacre fields. For the only time in all that winter Mr Milton was worried about them. "If they get trapped in the fields they will die," he said. Then another message came that they had broken back to the moor again. After that he did not worry about them. "They will be all right on Bradymoor," he said. He had faith in their ability to survive on the moor to which they were native.

In March I climbed up over the great drifts in Kitridge Lane – walking out over the end gate without knowing I had passed it – and walked out to see the shattered telegraph poles which had come down in the blizzards. And there I saw the ponies, all in a group, grazing upon a heathery patch from which the snow had blown fairly clear. I counted them, and they were all there. The next day I borrowed a camera and went back up to the moor and worked-up as near to the ponies as I could, and took some photos for a record. They were all in good condition. Though considerably thinned-down by the ordeal of enduring the worst winter in living memory, not one of them was in any way sick or sorry. As for the stallion, Forest, he was quite sleek, and looked in as good shape as might any hand-fed pony. So much for the wonderful hardiness of the true Exmoor.

Many tales are told of the ponies, past and present, but this chapter is growing over-long already. Why the ponies have the long hair of their tails cut off before being turned back to the Hill after the gathering should perhaps be recounted. Once, long ago, ponies did die on the moor, and it happened this wise: in a great blizzard of many years ago a group of ponies got trapped in the angle of the enclosure hedges just where the fields of Knighton and Brightworthy come together, and penned in by the hedges and the huge floundering drifts they starved. One pony only, a strong young stallion, managed to break out. He struggled down to Landacre Bridge, but as he went the snow balled up on his long tail until it became a huge block of ice, the weight of which eventually dragged him down, so that he too died. When he was found, his owner, an ancestor of the present Mr Milton, said that at least this should not happen again, and so since that time the ponies belonging to the Milton family have always had their tails shortened before the winter.

My own favourite memories of the herd upon the common are of Forest, Mr Milton's noble old stallion, who reigned upon the Hill for so many years. He was a true wild horse in every way, proud and unbroken, knowing only the open moor as home. He ruled his herd in proper style, keeping them together, warding them off the roads, driving them away from any point of danger or disturbance, and chasing off all intruders. I remember him once, a thing of dark red fury (he was bay) pursuing two large hunter geldings twice his size, who had somehow got out of their summer field onto the moor, and harrying them until they leapt in terror over a hedge and were off the common again. Woe betide any young stallion of any sort who presumed to approach any of old Forest's mares. The grand old boy gave them such a hiding that they fled and never came back again. I painted his portrait once. He got used to me being so often on the moor, and would let me approach quite close to himself and his family. He would never let himself be touched though – that would have been an indignity. The grand little horse is gone now, but his spirit and his stock live on, for the best ponies of recent years have been his children or his children's children, and some of them have gone far across the seas, to Denmark, to Norway, and to Canada.

CHAPTER ELEVEN

Hunting Days

Farming and hunting have always been the life of Exmoor. Man on Exmoor has, with few exceptions, ever been a farmer or a hunter, or both (though albeit often in the guise of a poacher), and farming and hunting still go hand in hand. The nature of the country makes it so. The wildness of the land, with its intermingling of high moor and deep wooded valleys, have made it a natural refuge for wild creatures, from the lordly red deer to the wily fox, whilst the pattern of pastoral farming likewise imposed by the terrain and climate have bred both a love of hunting and a necessity for it. Whether from the need to control the hill foxes who prey on the lambs in spring, or the deer who wreck the turnips in the winter, or from the desire to eat venison or to enjoy the exhilaration of a gallop on a good horse, hunting is part of the way of life for Exmoor folk, business and pleasure in one.

Withypool probably sees more hunting in a season than any other place in the country. Indeed it must be unique, for it stands at the junction of three hunting countries, four packs hunt across its land, and three of these packs actually meet in the village (and if one were to add the occasional visits of otter-hounds and beagles to those of the resident packs, one might bring the number of hunting packs up to six). So you see, Withypool is a very closely hunted parish.

The three hunting-countries that together converge upon Withypool bridge are respectively that of the Exmoor Foxhounds, which lies to the north and is bounded by the river and the main Comer's Cross road, that of the Dulverton West Foxhounds, which lies to the south of the river, and that of the Dulverton East Foxhounds, which lies to the east, and comes down to the bridge in a narrow wedge between the river and the Comer's Cross road.

The three packs which meet in the village are respectively the Exmoor Foxhounds, the Dulverton West, and the Devon and Somerset

Staghounds, in whose country the parish wholly lies. (The Dulverton East hold their meets for this corner of their country at Comer's Gate, just up above).

Hunting days! How one looks forward to them! How one scans the local paper for the "Hunting Appointments" column, hoping for meets that are on home ground, judging the distances of those that are farther afield, balancing the merits of such that occur on the same day. In this last, one so often has to make a definite choice, for inevitably two, perhaps three packs, are hunting on the same day, and their respective meets will be fairly equidistant and no more than a few miles off. (One has to reckon with getting to the meet, the probable draw and possible line of the run, and the getting home again afterwards). All this too, for nine months of the year, for with the summer staghunting and the Exmoor cubbing both beginning in August the hunting season extends from then until the end of April. There can be no other place so fortunate in this matter as Withypool.

Upon Exmoor the Devon and Somerset Staghounds take precedence over all other packs – this goes without saying – and when they honour us with a meet here in the village it is an event of local importance.

About half-past ten upon a morning in spring or autumn there is a sense of expectancy, a feeling of impending excitement in the air. Cars and Land Rovers, the first of many, begin to arrive and take suitable parking places. Folk come out of their houses and stand about talking. Eyes and ears are turned to the Exford road, for the hounds usually come early to take their stand before the appointed hour of eleven o'clock. The minutes slip by. Now there's a clatter of hooves on the road. They come – the glorious red coats, the big hounds, as fresh as paint, the horses tossing in the morning sun. How one's heart leaps to see them once again! They draw up outside the Royal Oak for a few minutes for a stirrup-cup and a few words, and then move on across the bridge to take their stand upon the corner of moor just opposite the village hall.

As the hour of eleven approaches, riders on horseback, led horses, and vehicles of every sort converge upon the village from every direction. Huge horse boxes push their way slowly along the narrow roads, edging their way carefully round corners, to finally stop and unload wherever convenient space affords itself. There's much stamping and trampling as the glossy-coated horses descend and fidget impatiently as they are saddled-up. All through the village cars are parked nose-to-tail wherever there is width enough to the road, and late-comers cruise slowly along, seeking some over-looked space, hoping that it will be one from which they will be able to extricate themselves without too much difficulty when the hounds move off. Those folk who have arrived per car separately from their horses now seek them, and either find them or wonder where the hell they are.

The hounds, drawn up on the patch of sward between the hedge and the rushes, are the cynosure of all eyes. Everyone throngs round, eager to see and appraise them. Those folk who have walked puppies pick them out now, and comment upon them, and are flattered if their hound remembers them. All the pack are aware of course that they are being admired, and seem almost to pose as the visitors take photos of them.

Further back the riders mill, fresh horses turning and tossing in the breeze that is always on the moor, all eager to be moving. The horses are always worth looking at, for there is no finer sight in all the world than a good horse well turned-out, and there are some very good horses in these parts. One sees all sorts as one casts one's eye around: Exmoor ponies, cobs whose mealy noses proclaim half Exmoor ancestry, small well-made hunters whose blood, one could guess, is quarter-Exmoor, bigger hunters of good breeding and quality, one or two real heavyweights and a few taller, more blood-like horses which one knows, or guesses, are point-to-pointers. On the whole though, neither very big horses nor blood-hunters are much seen. They are not suited to the country, which is rough and tough. A well-bred short-legged short-backed sort of about 15.2.hh. is perhaps the best mount one can have.

As for the riders, they are of all sorts too. Experienced riders who have known and ridden the moor all their lives, young ones who are learning its ways, two ladies on side-saddles (they are courageous, for this is not side-saddle country), children on ponies, a few visitors on hired horses – some who ride to hunt, and some who hunt to ride, but all are united in their love of horse and hound, the vigour of life and the wide world of the open air.

One sees though, as one looks around, and if one knows "the country" that most of the folk here, whether mounted on horseback or about to follow by car or Land Rover, are farmers and their families. For this is their country and their sport – at the time of writing both of the joint Masters are Exmoor farmers.

Meanwhile, Master, harbourer, and huntsman confer together concerning the whereabouts of a suitable stag. Most local folk have their own ideas, but we must wait for the Master to make his decision. At last there is a note of the huntsman's horn, and hounds move off. If our luck is in, and a huntable stag has moved into the coverts near to hand – Ham, Hayes, Kings or Oakbeer woods – then we shall see the deer turned out right here, but if not, then a long hack on to the Hawkridge coverts is most likely to be the order of the day. If the former, the pack will be kennelled in a horse box for the drawing of the tufters, if the latter, then they will go on to kennel most probably at Westwater, beyond

Greystone Gate.

Sometimes it is one way, sometimes the other, but always there's the excitement, the anticipation, the splendid cavalcade going away up the hill with ringing hooves, the joy of another hunting-morning. And the effort – one might almost say struggle – to get off to a good start, especially on the part of the car-followers, for whom delay and an error of judgement may mean being boxed-in in a traffic jam for an hour or so. Everyone naturally wants to get away to a vantage-point from whence they can watch the tufters drawing and hope to see the stag break, and admittedly road-risks are often taken which would not be justified by any other circumstances.

Other meets not far off, within a few miles, and from which the hunt may come back into the Withypool area, are to the east, Comer's Gate, the usual draw being the combes of the Winbrook, but with hounds almost always crossing over into the Barle; Winsford Hill, the actual meet being at Folly just on the Winsford side of the summit, the draw being either the Winbrook or the Allotments or the Tarr Steps coverts of the Barle; and Mounsey Hill Gate at the far end of Winsford Hill, whence, wherever the initial start, hounds almost always come over into the Barle at some stage. To the west, Sandyway is the near meet, the long coverts of the Mole being the harbour of the deer on that side, but hounds sometimes cross into the upper Barle by way of Sherdon. Southwards is Hawkridge itself, the thick coverts of the Barle and Dane's Brook on either side, and from the meets here one is almost certain to see and hear hounds working up the valley at some time in the day. To the north-east lies Exford, and when hounds meet there they almost always draw up the Exe valley under Room Hill, and occasionally come out over the top into Pennycombe. So you see, Withypool sees a fair share of the staghunting.

Of course one may see hounds at any time, suddenly and unexpectedly from any distant meet, as well as those near to hand, for long runs with points of ten miles or more are still to be had on occasion.

Withypool Hill itself is not infrequently crossed in the course of a run. Lord's Plantation just over at the back is a noted point for running deer, and the line is often up Westwater, or from the Dane's Brook, to Lord's, and then up over the top and down either Knighton Combe or Dillacombe to the upper Barle. Often from Withypool I have looked up to the top of the Hill, my eyes and ears called by the cry of hounds, and seen the hounds skimming across the heather, and the horsemen galloping along the skyline of the crest, moving as silhouettes against the light, with the sky under their horses' bellies, as stirring and exciting as any figures in a Wild West scene.

Sometimes the drama of the hunt comes closer than this, and galloping horsemen come careering through the village like a cavalry charge, hooves ringing in a mad tattoo (horses' legs seem to be made of iron in these parts – no-one ever pulls up for the tarmac), and everybody still at home comes flying out to their garden gates. I remember one occasion, not so very long ago, when the hunted stag came up the river and walked right through an arch of the bridge, continuing thence to Newland wood. On other occasions deer have run through gardens on either side of the village. Once a stag ran the length of the village street, but that was before my time and according to local remembrance. This past season of 1969 however, Withypool saw the latter part of a very long run, remarkable for its being of the Tiverton Staghounds, not the Devon and Somerset. The meet had been that morning at South Molton, and these hounds ran a stag right out of their own country, up over Withypool Hill and down to the Barle. The stag ran across the neck of moor along the south side of the village, crossed the river somewhere by Kings, to go out over Winsford Hill to the Winbrook. The hunt followers came on over the bridge and up the road, and eventually took their stag below Withycombe near Winsford. From South Molton to Withycombe is twelve miles flat on the map, not counting what twists and turns may have been made on route. It is the only time I have ever known the Tiverton Staghounds come into this country, and it was unusual to see the strange faces and strange horses going slowly home that night.

Many a good stag has come to his appointed end in the Barle between here and Hawkridge. The nearest finish I have known was the kill under Kings a few years ago, at the bend of the river just below the village. The next nearest was when a stag stood at bay at Southill stepping-stones. I remember the carcass being carried across the stepping-stones to the lane side with considerable difficulty, for the river was running very high at the time.

In winter, when hind-hunting takes the place of stag-hunting, the meets are smaller and all things less spectacular. The time of hind-hunting, from the middle of November to the end of February, is that of the hardest part of the year, and the sport is that of those local folk who are themselves hard and keen. Flooding rivers, impassable fords, bitter winds, snow, sleet and hard going, and short dark days are the general conditions to be contended with, especially after Christmas. The hunting itself can often be arduous. I recall one run, from Hawkridge to the Bray, the line of which was across Withypool Hill, which was of thirty miles as hounds ran. At this season meets are often held at farms and out-of-the-way places which would be unsuitable in spring and autumn. Westwater, just beyond Greystone Gate is one such place around here.

Next after the Devon and Somerset Staghounds, one may, in order of precedence, place the Exmoor Foxhounds, for they hunt over the greater part of high Exmoor. Foxhunting is in this country a primal necessity as well as being a great sport, for the hill-foxes are strong and wolf-like in their ways, and harass the lambing flocks in spring, ready to take the young lambs and even a ewe that is down and helpless.

Here, as with stag-hunting, we get our fair share of attention. When the Exmoor Foxhounds meet in Withypool, they do so outside the Royal Oak, with the hounds drawn up in the angle of the front, and a pretty picture they make. The scene and bustle in general is much the same as that of a meet of the staghounds, but on a lesser scale, for except in April, when all hunting reaches its zenith in an end-of-season climax, the meets tend to be small. They are more local affairs, with the killing of foxes in the immediate district the prime consideration.

When hounds move off, the first draw is usually the little copse and rough brake behind Garliscombe, and on to the combe between Weatherslade and Foxtwitchen, where foxes so often lie in the thicket of gorse and brambles on the far side. With luck a fox may be in the fern on the brake, and then everyone waiting below will get a grandstand view of the find. (I remember one occasion when a fox jumped up from behind the Mill Cleave green-house). With what eagerness we all wait, watching each hound that quests deeper into the rough, all tensed for the first sound, the opening cry that will proclaim a find, and for the exhilarating notes of horn that will tell of another hunting day truly begun.

From Weatherslade hounds may run out to Room Hill, where there are big earths, or they may come back into Pennycombe. An alternative first draw is Blindwell, on the side of Pennycombe itself, and another Newland Wood. But wherever they try first, almost always they come over into Pennycombe at some time of the day, for it is a veritable hive of foxes, or it used to be.

Another meet in the parish is Bradymoor Gate, of which I have already spoken, and from which the first draw, after a possible throw-off in the rushes, is usually Landacre Brake. Sometimes they meet at Pickedstones Gate, in the far corner of Bradymoor. Other meets near to hand, though just outside the parish, are Chibbet Post above Pennycombe, Honeymead further to the west, and occasionally Horsen beyond the upper river. Any one of these meets may bring the hounds back into the Withypool coverts, and it is seldom that one is out of earshot.

The Dulverton West, when they meet here in Withypool, take their stand at the bridge, just on the patch of grass at the south-west butt. They hunt Withypool Hill, where there are always foxes and their first draw is usually Knighton Combe. Sometimes though, they go into the river valley under Kings, drawing through the gorse above the drive en route, and if they find here, then again Withypool has a grandstand view.

Occasionally they meet at Landacre Bridge, and to see them there is a lovely sight. Greystone Gate is also an occasional meet, and beyond, more regularly, they meet at Westwater, Hawkridge, Willingford Bridge and Sandyway. They are a fine pack, hunting with great force and drive, and although their country is properly beyond the river, it is not at all uncommon for them to push a fox across the river into Exmoor country. Then we see the red coats with the dark green collars on this side, and horsemen galloping over the bridge and up the street as with the staghounds – for there are no good fords of the Barle between Withypool and Landacre Bridge.

The Dulverton East we see less, for when they meet at Comer's Gate they draw Winsford Hill, and seldom come right down into their wedge of land that runs into Withypool. They hunt the coverts of the Barle under Bradley of course, but usually go downstream. Like the Dulverton West, they have green collars to their coats.

In addition to these resident foxhound packs, we see the visiting Heythrop each April, when they come down to Exmoor by invitation after their season has finished in their own country. They bring with them something of up-country state, and their meets rival those of the staghounds. All who are able try to get a day out with the green coats, for they show great sport.

Now with all these packs hunting in so close an area inevitably at least two on the same days of the week, it is not infrequent for them to get mixed up on occasion. One may be following one pack, hear hounds and go to them, and then find that they are not the ones one started with! The packs themselves may even run into one another and get intermixed – I remember this happening once at Westwater when a mixed pack of stag and fox hounds had to be kennelled and sorted out! I don't know of any other part of England where this is likely to happen except on Exmoor.

As to hare-hunting, though hares are frequent, we have no resident pack of harehounds on the high moor. The Quarme Harriers, who used to hunt this district (they were kennelled at Exford) are no longer in existence. The Crowcombe Basset hounds seldom come this way now, but I have memories of them, and their wonderful cry, rivalling that of any foxhounds. Packs of beagles, though, occasionally visit us, and give a good scramble over the Hill.

In the summer the otter hounds occasionally meet here in Withypool, and draw along the Barle, but I confess I have never been out with them. Somehow, the time of kingcups and may-blossoms does not seem proper for hunting.

The hunting season on Exmoor ends in fine style, with numerous point-to-points, each pack holding its own. Our nearest is that of the Dulverton East, at Venford, five miles off, just beyond Hawkridge. Both the Exmoor and the Dulverton West hold theirs at Bratton Down, over in Devon, and the Devon and Somerset at Holnicote in Porlock Vale. To all of these most folk around here manage to get by one means or another, and for the enthusiasts there are others not very much further off. By the time one has been to half-a-dozen between March and May one has had a fair fill of racing as well as hunting. Who says country life is dull?

CHAPTER TWELVE

Of Gardening, and the Flower Show

Withypool folk are fond of their gardens and proud of their abilities to garden well under the conditions of the locality, as indeed they should be, for the terms imposed by this high moorland region are far from easy. What is ultimately achieved may be seen and judged at that culmination of the horticultural effort, the annual Withypool Flower Show, which takes place about the third week of each August.

Gardening is a subject after my own heart, and as I have been a gardener all my life, and since being in Withypool have always cultivated a garden in one part or another, I feel able to write at length and with first-hand knowledge of the subject.

To begin with the first things first, which are for the gardener – as indeed for the farmer and all others in actual fact – climate and soil, one may say that the climate is predominately a wet and windy one, and the soil, once reclaimed from its original moorland peat-surface state, a fairly light loam over shillet, in general of an acid nature. The altitude being high – Withypool in the valley is over the 900 feet mark, whilst cultivation in various parts of the parish goes up to 1200 feet – the spring, because of this, is very late. This is counterbalanced however by a long-drawn out autumn. The land being everywhere hilly, most gardens are on a slope, so naturally drain well despite the rain. Very late spring frosts are a hazard, but the incidence of frost varies. I have often known a garden high on a hill escape the blasting of a late frost whilst Withypool in its valley by the river was severely struck by it. The latest frost I have known in these parts is June 7th. In general conditions are healthy and disease minimal.

So one may say one's advantages here are fresh pure air, free-draining soil, onto which one can get almost as soon as it stops raining, and a long open autumn in which one seldom gets a killing frost until November, with little hard weather in general until after Christmas.

The disadvantages, one's chief enemies as it were, are the battering winds, the often incessant rain (though with free-drainage this is not so serious), a tendency to leaching in the soil, and the generally cold late spring. But taking all in all, the good and the bad balance fairly well, and once one gets to understand the ways of the hill-country, and get the "feel" of things it is wonderful what one can do with any patch of ground around here.

A typical hill-country garden is one of about four square rods or more, set in the sunniest possible position, and enclosed by high earthen banks that are designed to be both stock and wind-proof.

All Exmoor dwellings, whether farmhouse or cottage, have attached to them such a garden, but this garden is not always immediately adjacent to the house, being often a little distance away, on the other side of a farmyard or across a lane. The purpose of the garden being strictly utilitarian, for the growing of vegetables, soil and sun are more important than visual display, and the fact that one cannot see the garden except when one is actually in it is an unimportant matter. A garden-patch around the house for the pleasure of flowers which one can see from one's windows is something quite different, and an idea which has gained ground only in comparatively recent times, at least on the farms. (After all, sheep and bullocks and free-range poultry don't exactly make good companions for delicate flowers). Here in the village, however, we have both sorts of garden, or gardens which fulfil both functions, and so combine practicality with pleasure.

We have indeed gardens of all kinds. Big gardens and small gardens. Steep gardens and (almost) flat gardens. Terraced gardens and plain gardens. Gardens that are mainly for the growing of vegetables and gardens that are given over to the growing of flowers. In short, gardens that are of all sorts according to all the different tastes and needs of gardeners.

Since Withypool is set in the main on a hillside – or three hillsides to be correct, for there are a number of dwellings on the south side of the river and several on the rise beyond the Pennycombe – sloping gardens naturally predominate, only the comparative few which are on the valley floor being really flat. So with fall of ground and change of level prevailing in most gardens, some sort of terracing with walling and steps is a local feature. Here the 'dyking' or 'ditching' of the hill-country comes into its own, many of the gardens having banks and walls of this essentially Exmoor construction. Such work properly done presents a beautiful texture of natural stone, and lends itself to an "alpine" sort of planting. Steps and stepping-stones are made of big slabs of blue slate, and ferns automatically grow in the crevices, and one may even have a spring of clear water channelled through the garden to fall over ledges. So altogether the local style does indeed truly reflect in itself and in small compass the character of the moor.

My own little back garden begins at a level some eight feet above that of the tiny yard, and is approached by way of a flight of ten steep stone steps from just beside the back door. (Literally a case of going upstairs to garden!) From its beginning it slopes gradually upwards, so that on turning round at the top I can look back over the roof of my own dwelling to the fields and the long dark line of the moor. The slope is to the south, and there is a wall and a high hedge to the north, stopping the coldest winds, so my little patch is always full of sunshine, and I know how these hillside gardens clasp and hold the spring warmth when it comes, and in their haven produce the loveliest of flowers and the richest of strawberries. So much joy this little patch of precious earth has given me, with its tiny lawn upon which to sit and look out to the Hill, its pretty flowers to rejoice eyes and heart, and its good fruit and vegetables to eat. Though I now have a much bigger piece of ground in hand a little way off, this is still my especial patch, my 'sitting place' and my nursery where I rear my young plants.

As to what one can grow in this district, one can in fact grow most things if one is patient and considerate to the plants, but naturally some things do better than others. Taking flowers and shrubs first, since these are the most obvious, those that flourish best and really do well are, naturally enough, those that like peaty or acid lime-free soil and a high altitude: rhododendrons, azaleas, heaths and heathers, alpines of all sorts, primulas, and members of the viola family. (One might add hydrangeas, were it not that Withypool is a bit too frosty for them, for on the east side of the moor they grow luxuriantly).

Rhododendrons and azaleas, once established, grow with great abandon, and when the season suits them put forth such a show of bloom as I do not think any place in the world can surpass. I have recollections of such plants where they grow grouped together uplifting to the intense blue sky of an Exmoor spring massed heads of crimson, magenta, white, pink, orange and yellow, in an exotic blaze of colour that almost bewilders the senses.

This is by nature heather country, and all heaths and heather do well once they too are established, and fit most properly into the style of banks and walling that here prevails, giving bloom from February onwards to the autumn. The early spring heaths are especially a delight. The tussocks of lovely pink and mauve topping the banks and walls of weathered grey stone, companion to the drifts of snowdrops, all under the bare branches of the yet-sleeping winter trees, are like a gift out of autumn to the beginning of the year, a promise of all the later glory. And what is more lovely than a few sprigs intermingled with a bunch of early primroses? With regard to planting, it is a curious fact that these "Mediterranean" heaths seem easier to establish in a garden than the native sorts. The native heather – all three species of it – is obstinate, self-willed and uncooperative. I look across my boundary wall at a thousand acres of it, flourishing in wild abandon on the Hill, but it doesn't want to grow in my garden, or in anyone else's. In almost every case I know where transplanting has been attempted, it has sulked and refused to be tamed. Well, one must respect it for its independence – in so many ways it is the emblem of freedom.

Obstinacy and temperament bring one to the gentians. When and where gentians choose to grow in an Exmoor garden they do so with almost the vigour and prolificness of weeds. (I have seen in some gardens what I can only describe as mats of *Gentiana acaulis*, so laden with flowers of peacock-blue as to make one's eyes blink). But they will only grow how, when, and where they please. I remember the late owner of Dadhays used to have the most lovely gentians along the front border by the roadside, but when she moved to a house scarcely more than a hundred yards away, and took her treasures with her, they refused to flourish there, though to all intents the soil was just – or almost – the same. With other alpines the tale is somewhat similar – they will either grow wonderfully well or not at all.

The primula tribe, however, are most obliging and without prejudices. They love the district (see the wild primroses on any scrubby slope) and will grow almost anywhere with relish. Coloured primroses, gay polyanthus, round-headed blue primulas – tall three-tiered candelabra primulas – they all flourish, and collectively give a splendid display of bloom from late March to early June. They seed like mad too, and are easily raised from seed. A friend had a perfect sapphire-blue primrose appear from nowhere in her hedge, which she has now transplanted to a position of pride in the main bed. In my own little garden, under the top hedge, I had a "Jack in the Green" come up most mysteriously. It appeared as a seedling, and flowering the next year gave me the greatest possible surprise: every butter-coloured flower had a little ruff of green leaves about its neck like a collar. I still cherish it, and have given cuttings to several friends, but I have no idea where it could have come from, since I had never had any such plant before, nor know of anyone else in the neighbourhood who possessed one. In the deliberate raising of polyanthus from seed, that is in a seed-box, I have had as many as seventy plants from the pinch of seed sown – which must have represented almost every seed in the packet. Yet some people tell me they are difficult to raise from seed. Mine were only planted in ordinary garden soil.

So I come now to pansies. How I love them, and how well they do grow hereabouts. To speak from my own experience, I can best give praise to them by describing the results I had last year from one ninepenny packet of Carter's seeds bought at the Post Office. The tale actually begins the preceding year, when I got the packet and sowed the seed in a seed-box in early summer. From that box I planted out over seventy seedling plants, and they flowered that autumn in September. The following spring – that of last year – they began to bestir themselves at the end of March (despite the extreme lateness of the spring of 1969), and to flower in April. What they did from then onwards was quite incredible. They grew and grew until they became bushes knee-high (the packet said six inches – I have it still), smothered with blooms as big round as cups and of every possible colour – wine-red, fire-red, purple, mauve, sapphire blue, pink, white and yellow – and all with the sweetest of scent. By June the bushes had reached a height of nearly two feet six inches, and then we had some high winds which flattened them, but after that they rose again and stood up to two feet high, at that time I got a witness to come and measure them, for a record. And all this growth was made without any abatement of flowering. They continued to literally flower their heads off right through to October, the only concession being that the blooms became somewhat smaller as time went on. They gave me more than six months continuous flowering before withdrawing for the winter. At first I tried to cut off the dead heads to conserve the strength of the plants, but I could not keep pace with them, and had to let them go their own way. Consequently they have seeded all over the place, and made themselves into a thicket. What the results will be this year, I don't know. So much for pansies in the hill-country.

This past autumn I raised and planted-out a patch of violas (at least the packet said they were violas – I never know the difference between a pansy and a viola), and am now waiting eagerly to see the first flowers.

A friend just down the road has the most wonderful violas in her garden, the range of colours including scarlet, sky-blue, and orange, and so I am hoping for equal things.

Another plant which goes quite mad here is the forget-me-not. It grows and flowers in clouds of blue wherever you will let it, and seeds like mustard-and-cress all over the place. It happily fills all spaces between all other plants.

Spring bulbs of every sort do well here. Snowdrops, crocus, daffodils, narcissus, tulips and hyacinths – the cottage gardens are full of them in succession from the interludes of sun in February to the warmer days of June. As to the flowers of summer, a whole galaxy present themselves. Climbing roses that ramble round windows in a profusion of blooms as big as tea-cups, anchusa blue as the sky, sweet scented wallflower, sweet williams, columbines, delphiniums, iris, lilies, Canterbury bells, nemesias, musk, lovely pink or white tall anemones – well, more or less everything. With the autumn comes a blaze of dahlias and Michaelmas daisies, and finally the glow of the berried shrubs. Even things which one would not expect to take kindly to the hill-country – such as irises – do in fact flourish if treated with sympathy.

Coming back to more native growth, it goes without saying that ferns of every sort delight in this country. By nature they grow in every crevice (and not only out-of-doors – I know of places where they sprout from the cracks of interior walls), intermingling with the mosses and lichens and achieving frond sizes from a few inches to several feet. If one wishes to have a fern-garden, then this is the place for it.

To come to more practical things: that is, the growing of vegetables. As with flowers, most sorts will do well enough, but some are easier and some more difficult. Potatoes are a good crop, and generally free from disease, so that one can save one's own "seed". This year I took four hundred-weight off one square rod of ground (varieties Catriona, Majestic and Dunbar Standard), which is pretty fair going. It is a curious thing, generally recognized by gardeners in the district, that crops grown from seed-potatoes themselves grown in local soil are better and heavier than the crops from fresh "up country" seed. Hence it is a general practice to save one's own "seed" which has become acclimatized.

Swedes, turnips, and parsnips and beetroot are no trouble, but carrots are difficult. Leeks and shallots are easy, but onions awkward, though I do know one local gardener who has the genius to grow the biggest and finest onions I have ever seen. For ordinary folk, growing from "sets" is the best bet. The brassica tribe all do well enough if started off early, though I find that "spring cabbages" will not over-winter – those that survive all want to bolt with the coming of spring. Of the leguminosae, both broad beans and runner-beans do exceedingly well, but peas are something of a nightmare in their early stages, for everything around here that eats preys upon them. However, if one can get them up to the flowering stage, then they crop very well. Indeed, they do extremely well: this past summer my row of peas, the packet of which said "four feet six inches", grew to over seven feet (again I have a witness for this statement), and was so laden with pods that it had to be reinforced with bean-poles.

Almost everything else that one can think of, from celery to seakale, will flourish given due care, and as for rhubarb, it will reach giant proportions.

As to fruit, all "bush fruits" – gooseberries, currants, raspberries etc. – will grow and bear prolifically, but the best of all rewards for the fruit-lover in these parts is a good strawberry bed. Strawberries grow magnificently here. Planted out on a sunny sheltered slope, just a small bed will provide you with more strawberries than you can eat in a day (breakfast, dinner, tea, and supper – I speak from experience), for more than three weeks, and with a succession of varieties you can make a glutton of yourself for about three months. I have at the moment five varieties, but of all these my favourite is still Royal Sovereign – in flavour, colour, form, scent, and free-cropping it is still the very king of strawberries. Strangely though, not a great many people around here do seem to grow strawberries. Yet they are no trouble to grow – just put them in and they root and wax strong at once, and fight the weeds on their own level. But perhaps in this last there is a hint of trouble: I do not know what the general behaviour of strawberries in other people's gardens may be, but here in mine the ultimate aim of all, even the noblest varieties, is to go wild. They throw out runners faster than any sane person can cut them, and race away yards from where they started, invading all other beds devoted to other things, diving under hedges, climbing over rockeries, getting a stranglehold on more delicate plants, and generally establishing themselves everywhere. In next to no time one has a strawberry jungle instead of a garden. So with praise of strawberries one must also add the warning that they need a strong hand.

Apples will not grow, or at least only very poorly. It is the same all over high Exmoor – it is not apple-country, and apples just don't want to grow. Some keen gardeners persist in trying, and periodically plant trees, but these never seem to come to anything. There are, I believe just five apple trees in the parish, but whether they ever have apples on them, I don't know. Not until one comes to the lower fringes of the moor does one find orchards.

Plums of the damson type do tolerably well (as they should, considering the wild sloes that abound), but the larger sorts not very well.

Pears I have never heard of in the district, but doubt if they would do any better than the apples. "Flowering" cherry trees make a lovely show of pink and white blossom in the village in the spring, but I do not know of any bearing edible cherries. Cultivated sorts of cob or filbert type might flourish, seeing that the wild hazel is so prolific all around, but I do not know of anyone who has tried to establish these.

As to general cultivation, the local soil needs constant nourishment. Everyone has their own methods. I myself am a compost-fiend, making as much as I can with every sort of animal and vegetable substance I can get hold of. On the evidence of overall practical results I am prepared to back my method against anyone else's – but that is another story. Opinion is divided upon whether to sow early or late. Some folk do not sow until May (this being the equivalent of April or earlier in lower country), others try to get things away to an early start by raising plants in a greenhouse. (Blessed are they who have a greenhouse – I have not). I try to make a first sowing of hardy things at the end of March if there is a suitable fine interval in the weather, and also raise seedlings in boxes on my bedroom windowsills. Early May is on the whole the best time for putting in maincrop things on open ground. Pests are an unpleasant subject, but must in all honesty be mentioned. Disease and blight seldom trouble the gardener here, but the larger predators that eat certainly do. The principal garden pests of this region are slugs, field-mice, sparrows, wood-pigeons and rabbits, and moving up the scale in size one cannot exclude sheep and cattle as possible decimators – one must always make sure one's fences are stock-proof, and one's gates securely fastened, in this pastoral country. Against all these aforementioned pests one must fight an unceasing battle, and as every gardener knows, it is war without mercy or quarter from the moment the first seed goes in.

No survey of local gardening would be complete without mention of the greenhouse-culture that goes on. Our keenest gardeners have greenhouses, some of them heated, and within are grown all manner of fine things from tomatoes and cucumbers to the most exotic flowers. What a little moorland village can produce of its soil, all in all, is truly amazing.

If you would see the sum total, the climax of all this horticultural effort and activity, however, you must come to the Flower Show.

The Flower Show is Withypool's Big Day, something that is planned and worked for from the beginning of the year. About the middle of August activity is to be noted about the small green meadow that lies between the river and the road, just opposite the Post Office. Grass is being cut short and smooth, tents erected, mysterious courses laid out, bunting hung over the gate. Up the hill, in the Village Hall, trestle-tables are being ranged with practised skill. The Day is at hand.

Upon the actual morning – it is usually the third Wednesday in August – all the village is in a bustle. All good folk are hurrying up the hill to the Hall where the actual Flower Show is staged, carrying their numerous exhibits to the benches. There are many classes, for all sorts of things as well as flowers, and it is incumbent upon all good citizens to do something for the Flower Show. Ten o'clock, and the first rush is over, the Hall being closed for judging. We can all relax until the afternoon. But we don't. All eyes watch the weather. A fine afternoon is so vital. If it is wet, we pray for a break in the clouds. If it is fine, then we watch apprehensively for approaching signs of rain. Happy is the day that is cloudless and full of sunshine!

By half-past two the village and the road up to the Hall is full of cars, Land Rovers and folk on foot, all converging on the Hall itself, and a crowd is gathering about the entrance. At last, some public person having made a formal opening speech, the Show is open, and we may enter.

What colour, what splendid visions greet the eye! Every inch of the benching is full of flowers, vegetables, and handcraft exhibits. The classes seem endless – for cut flowers, flower arrangements, foliage, pot-plants, vegetables of all sorts, needlework, knitting, cakes, scones, jam, eggs, children's drawing and handwriting competitions. Everyone circulates round and round, eager to see who has the prizes, and pass comment with neighbours. After about two circuits one comes away with a confused recollection of gladioli, dahlias, sweet-peas, roses, pansies, begonias and every other sort of summer flower, all intermingled in one's mind with iced cakes and brown eggs, potatoes and embroidered cushion-covers, cauliflowers and school watercolours. It is indeed a marvellous show for one small moorland parish, (though in this Hawkridge is included, and Great and Little Ash, and also Sandyway), and the judges never fail to comment upon the very high standard of the exhibits, especially of the horticultural side. One of the memories, or impressions, that I always carry away from the Show is that of the extreme contrast between the view from the south-west windows of the Hall, of the moor, bleak and primaeval, and the display upon the benches within of the lovely luxurious flowers in all their glory of colour. So does the wilderness truly blossom as the rose under the hand of loving care.

Having seen the main display in the Hall, one now adjourns to the sports field and tea-tent down by the river. Here one consumes tea, cake, and buttered scones, and meets old friends – for the Flower Show is a great social occasion, to which all persons in the parish come, and to which return former residents who have moved to other parts but whose hearts are still here under the shadow of the moor. Then a tour of the other stalls and side-shows fills in time, and by the early evening the children's sports are under way. There's plenty of enthusiasm, energy and excitement from the young, and when at last all the races are run the day's proceedings usually end with some home-made spectacle such as a comic football match between the youth of Withypool and Hawkridge. So another Flower Show day closes, with, one hopes, good takings for the Village Hall fund.

A brave display, from beginning to end, and one of which to be proud.

CHAPTER THIRTEEN

Snow

So far, this winter of writing, we have had very little snow, though it being only February we may yet have plenty. Here in the hills our winter does not properly begin – or seldom so – until after Christmas, and our spring cannot be expected until the end of April, possibly not until May. The seasons are late here. Candlemas Day (February 2nd), rather than either December 21st or January 1st, marks our mid-winter, and we can expect harder weather after this date than before. "As the days lengthen so doth the cold strengthen" says one old saying, and "Till Candlemas Day keep half your hay" says another. Both are wise, and born of experience.

Snow is a word nobody likes to use in these parts until they have to. Heavy snow is the dread of the hill-farmer, for even with the best precautions it can mean being cut off in isolation for weeks, perhaps months, and possibly the death of many head of stock. In general, our winters are not severe, for the proximity of the ocean and the consequent prevalence of what is called an "Atlantic climate" gives us wet weather rather than cold, with days of mist and driving rain rather than ice and frost, but nevertheless snow comes sooner or later, and when it does it falls heavier, drives harder and lies longer than upon the lower ground. A few hours' snow upon a driving wind at this altitude is enough to choke every lane, block every gateway, and bury as many sheep as are not well looked-to. With a heavy fall the narrow high-banked lanes pack full to hedge-height, whilst to attempt to face a blizzard on the open moor is a terrifying experience which one does well to avoid.

Snowfalls may come any time here from the middle of November onwards, and be quite heavy, but I have never known the snow to lie for more than a few days before Christmas. It is after Christmas that one can expect bad weather to set in. Though I cannot remember an actual "white Christmas" I have known it turn-in for snow on more than one Boxing Day. New Year parties and dances always have to be arranged with one eye on the weather – snow means they have to be cancelled, for folk gathered together at the onset of a snowstorm may very well be snowed-up and unable to get home within a few hours' time.

March is a month in which one can get, and usually expects, heavy falls of snow. April too can be a time of winter here, though the sun being fairly high by then, the snow is unlikely to lie very long. The latest date on which I have known a really severe blizzard is April 14th. This was in 1966, and many ewes and lambs were lost then, it being the middle of the lambing season. The snow lay for a week, and on April 20th the snow-ploughs were still battling through the head-high drifts "out over". On high ground there were drifts blocking the gateways right to the very end of the month. Even in May one may have snow on the hill-tops, but seldom more than flurries lower down. Folk tell, though, of a heavy fall once, years ago, which came late, and lay all through May, and was not quite gone till June, and how, on Midsummer's Day there was still some lying in Kitridge Lane.

But when one talks of snow, and reckons in terms of severity, it is of the great winter of 1963 that one thinks. This, in the opinion of almost everyone, was the most severe in living memory, considerably worse in general than even that of 1947, and its casualties less only because of the helicopter rescues. Certainly the winter of 1963 is one which I shall never forget.

It began on Boxing Day, 1962. I had been living away for a while, and having spent Christmas "out over", returned to Withypool on the afternoon of the said Boxing Day. When I arrived here it was already snowing – I was lucky to get back. Had I left it for another day I should not have got here at all.

By the next morning we had had a considerable fall, and it was still snowing. It snowed for seven weeks. To the best of my remembrance there was not a day when it did not snow in all that while. The ground of old England we did not see again for three months.

With the snow came bitter raging north-east winds, driving the unceasing snow into great drifts. In a short while all the roads and lanes were choked and all isolated places completely cut off, and after the first week there were S.O.S.'s from many lonely farms for help. Then the helicopters came, and what they accomplished is a saga in itself.

Those of us who were strong and able-bodied did what we could to help. I managed to get up to Lower Blackland two or three times a week to take bread and groceries and such mail as came in to the Sloley family. Sometimes I went with John Blackmore or another man, who had to get to the higher farm to see to stock (there was no-one living at Higher Blackland that winter), and sometimes I went alone. Knowing all the fields, and how the snow drifted and lay, I was always able to get there and back. But it was not really safe or sensible to go about alone in the teeth of such blizzards and deep snow as we had – even the men tended to pair-off when they tried to get through to outlying farms. My next-door neighbour was at the time struggling to get up to Weatherslade each day to help Mr Fred Milton, who was then on his own at the farm, so I took to going up with her, so that there were two of us together to come down home in the dark. Mornings I went to Blackland, I went as early as I could, so that I was able to go up to Weatherslade before midday each day. So the winter passed, day by day, effort by effort, and none of it I shall ever forget.

The memories come back, now as I write, and I feel I am living those days over again.

I remember the great stillness of the early mornings, with only the moan of the wind for sound, and no movement of life or machine to stir the white dawn. Only the muffling blanket of the snow enveloping everything, and snow still falling, falling. Then with the daylight the reassuring sound of a helicopter somewhere overhead, manifesting itself with its peculiar throbbing as it passed on one of its errands of mercy. Then later, usually towards dusk, the drone of the snow-ploughs as they struggled to break through to us by way of Winsford and Comer's Cross.

The snow-ploughs had a thankless, hopeless task. They worked day and night – often we could see the glare of their headlights afar off – but as often as they cut a way through, the cut filled in again almost at once. Sometimes they did manage to open a way right down Quarry Head into the village, and then supplies got into the village on wheels – once by police Land Rover and once per fire-engine – but mostly they were able only to keep Ash Lane open, and the men of Withypool had to get up to Comer's Cross on foot to bring down bread, meat and mail. On one occasion they made a big sledge and harnessed a horse and returned in triumph to have their photographs taken outside the Post Office. But the peculiar texture of the snow made things too difficult for even this, and in the end boots and sacks were the only general means of conveyance.

Even getting about on foot was extremely difficult at first, for the snow was as fine as powder, and as dry, and would not "pack", but remained loose and shifting, so that one could not get up on the top of it. One just sank into it, and floundered, and was in danger of being engulfed and smothered if one got into a drift. After a few weeks however, with the increasing cold and pressure, it did harden considerably, and one was able to walk over the drifts – with care, anyway.

Withypool itself, from its sheltered position under hills cutting off the north and east winds, escaped the full force of the blizzards and the snow did not drift too heavily here. Folk were able to dig each other out, and make ways from doors and garden gates to the focal-point of the Post Office. (How glad we were for a well-stocked stores!) However, it was bad enough – the snow was waist-deep in my back yard.

Outside the village, the drifts were tremendous, rising up everywhere in great curving billows, arched at the tops like waves of the ocean about to break over one's head as one walked under them. Every lane was choked up to its hedge-roots (which in these parts is a depth of five or six feet), and some to their very hedge-tops, and every field gate was buried out of sight. In half-sheltered places the snow formed fantastic sculptures of itself, but in the open it did not cling to the trees, for the piercing winds did not allow it to settle, and the hedges for the most part stood black-topped above the drifts.

I remember it growing colder and colder, with an intensity of cold that had to be experienced to be believed. (What the temperatures might have dropped to on those January nights, I don't know, for no-one had any time or thought for a thermometer – we were all too busy just trying to keep ourselves and our beasts alive). Everything in creation froze: eggs in the larder (which burst with the cold), milk in the jug, meat in the safe, plants in pots, all taps and pipes, and even the water-main underground in parts. Every morning was a battle to try and thaw things out, especially the water-taps. I often used snow melted-down over the stove rather than bother. On the coldest nights of all, in mid-January, the frost came right through the walls of my cottage and glittered in the lamplight and killed my geraniums right down to the roots though they were stood by the stove all night.

Then the river froze, the swift Barle which in ordinary winters runs too fast and strong to fetter with ice. It froze right over in one thick sheet, and was still at last. Then for a few days there was a semblance of winter sports, with the young folk sliding and playing on the ice, and one gentleman who possessed skates giving a good show of figure-skating. But in a short while the surface of the ice was snowed over, and the river was as a long white road traversing the valley.

There was very little sun to hearten one through the long bitter winter.

Some bright sunny interludes we did get between the snowstorms, but they were all too few. There were none of the long clear blue-skyed days such as one usually gets after heavy snow, or at least I don't remember them. Mostly the snow-cloud was too prevalent, and it was all grey sky, white snow, and icy wind.

I remember the long hours of battling with the snow. I was out in it from early morning to after dark every day. Both Lower Blackland and Weatherslade are extremely difficult farms to get to in time of snow, on account of their both being set on hills, each with a steep combe intervening in the line of approach from the village. I remember the wind, so cold and piercing that the bite of it was like a burn. If one turned to face it, it cut off one's breath as though an icy hand were clapped over one's face. I remember the snow pouring over every gateway and through every gap like smoke from a great white fire. I remember when it was not possible to face it, and to get through the gap I had to turn around and struggle backwards.

I remember the constant struggle of each day. The zig-zagging across the fields spade in hand, to find and follow the lie of the drifts, and the digging through when there was no other way, only to have one's path filled-in again by the next morning. The struggle just to keep stock alive. The digging out of sheep, the attempts to dig out gateways, the cutting through of drifts up to ten feet deep to get at stock or move them. The back-breaking carrying of bales of hay and straw and oaten-sheaves out to both sheep and cattle (no tractor could move in such snow, and though we made a sledge of sorts on one occasion, it proved more trouble than it was worth). The constant attempts to smash ice over the drinking-places of the cattle – for whereas sheep seem able to do without water in winter, and ponies will mouth snow or crack ice for themselves, cattle seem stupid and need water to be provided. The attempts to clean-out shippons wherein the dung froze to the floor as it dropped. The daily spading of turnips for the sheep: at Weatherslade Mr Milton had as usual a good field of Scotch green-and-purple-topped turnips, this particular winter on the highest field of the farm, 1200 feet up on Room Hill, and having cut our way up there on a tour of inspection we found the wind had blown the snow away to a depth of a mere foot or eighteen inches for an acre or so, so we set-to and dug out a rap for the ewes each morning. Then we drove them up there through the cuts we had made for a few hours, and then brought them down again before nightfall, to a field judged fairly safe (that is from the worst drifting). The turnips, incidentally, were in excellent condition under their covering of snow, and we had a good supply for our own vegetable needs, too. There were times, too when we also went gunning for foxes.

All these chores collectively took until long after dark. Then at last there came the hot evening meal at the farmhouse for us humans, and the supreme relaxation of a sit by the fire. Finally there was, for my friend and myself, the last great effort of the day, the effort to turn out into the intense cold of the night and go down to our respective homes in the village. The distance was only about a mile, but dog-tired as we were, and with the bitterness of the wind to face, it took us all of our will-power to do it.

So the days of January passed, one day after another. They were the hardest I have ever known. I do not, however, recall on any occasion feeling actual bodily cold – rather the reverse, for the constant effort and exertion of moving about in the deep snow set one sweating under one's heavy clothing, and even hands and feet kept warm in thick gloves and Wellington boots. The one vulnerable part was one's face. Despite headscarf and sou'wester, one could not keep the cold from the face. All the while one had to be on one's guard against frost-bite, and to stop and rub nose and cheeks whenever one sensed a numbness. Even one's breath froze on the edges of one's scarf.

Then came the great February blizzard. This, one of the greatest snowstorms ever known in the West Country, came upon a changing wind, upon the night of the first Tuesday of the month. The wind went round to the south-east, and there was a lessening of the cold and with it an ominous heaviness. By dusk it was snowing with greater intensity than before, and by about eight o'clock that night the wind had risen to gale-force. All that could be seen in the light from the farmhouse windows was a whirling mass of white. But we had to go home – my neighbour had animals of her own down in the village to be looked to – and the longer we delayed the worse the conditions were likely to become. Mr Milton did not like us going, and bade us keep shoulder to shoulder and not part company for one moment. So we set out. It was I think the worst walk I have ever had, and an experience I have no wish to repeat. The blizzard was coming up almost due south, and straight into our faces. The snow was already building up into a muffling mass all round. Torches were useless. All we could do was to plunge on, steering by instinct, and hope for the best. At last we got down to the bottom of the fields and into the village. I have never felt more thankful to be home. I think we were both pretty exhausted. Looking back, I think we were lucky – if the wind had been as cold as it was in January, or our way uphill instead of down, we should not have made it.

Next morning we awoke to such a world of snow as I have never seen before, or expect to see again. Everything everywhere was just buried under a deep muffling blanket of white. When I got outside the back door it seemed in general to be about waist-deep, though where the wind had scooped it, it was less. The snow had stopped falling, and one could look about, and see the drifts piled everywhere. I saw my friend, and our first thought was for the farm and the beasts. It seemed hopeless to get up to Weatherslade, but we made up our minds to try. Somehow, digging and struggling and floundering waist-deep, we managed it. The snow in the yard was about four feet deep, and in the fields beyond we could see giant drifts. Mr Milton made us drink cups of hot strong tea laced with brandy, and then we set off to find the sheep. Mr Milton had put them the evening before in the one field where he said they would not bury, from the juxtaposition of the hedges with the direction of the wind. All the morning we dug and dug, and at last broke through the huge drifts to the sheep field – Little Bottom Field I remember it was named. "Maister" called, and sheep-voices answered. There they were, in the middle of the field, all of them, and none buried, though the drifts rose like great walls all round.

Later, when I was able to get up to Lower Blackland, I found the Sloley family had saved their flock that night by bringing them into a small field by the house and staying up with them all night, stirring them and keeping them moving all the while, so that they continuously trampled the snow under foot and kept above it. But the losses on many farms were grievous, and it was something no-one liked much to talk about.

Meanwhile, the village itself was quite cut off. Telegraph poles and wires were down. The snow-ploughs themselves were buried under the drifts. So the helicopters came, and kept us alive. The little field behind the school was designated the landing-ground, and the school Union Jack set up as a marker-flag. All the village came out to see the 'dragon-fly' touch-down, and the strongest to plunge through the snow to take off the bread, meat, and other emergency supplies which it brought.

When we – that is, us Weatherslade folk – were able to get up to the top fields again, we found the Room Hill Road buried under an almost unbelievable depth of snow. We walked out onto it from the field, over a hedge the topmost twigs of which just showed here and there above the snow, else we would not have known it existed. We estimated the depth of packed snow along the length of the road to be about twelve feet. (Subsequent measurement of the hedge-height after the snow had finally gone confirmed this as accurate).

When first fallen it must have been far more than this. Turning round and looking back to the moor, we could see only smooth snow where the head of Knighton Combe had been. It was quite blotted-out. What the depth of snow packed into the combe might have been, we did not dare to guess.

After about a week, by a superhuman effort, a gang of men digging, accompanied by the snow-ploughs, managed to break through to Withypool via Comer's Cross. The drifts there, they said, were twenty feet high.

After this great February blizzard not much more snow fell. Underfoot, the lying snow settled down to become harder, and one could get about much better, walking over the top of the drifts.

As the days lengthened, I got more adventurous. I walked up to Bradymoor, and it was there that I saw the ponies (see chapter 10). I saw also the telegraph poles: every one of them had been snapped off about a foot from the ground, as though some giant hand had plucked them and thrown them out over the moor to lie in a welter of wires and splinters.

I walked up to Comer's Gate, and the drifts there appeared as the great pyramids of Egypt, still about twenty feet high. They must have been far greater when first formed. I also walked to Sandyway and found the drifts still up to the eaves of the inn in places. They had been up to the chimney-tops, I was told, and I can readily believe it.

I tried in my peregrinations to make a few odd sketches, and succeeded with one or two. My friend and neighbour, who had a camera, had been taking photos whenever she could all through the winter, and so between us we had a good record of 1963 in all its phases.

By late March snow on the middle of most of the fields had blown or wilted away, and one could see ground again. But the great drifts remained, like white walls everywhere.

It seemed that nothing could shift them. They just jammed down harder and harder. Spire Rocks lane was full of frozen snow right up to the tips of the picket-fence that runs along the top of the north-east bank, and no snow-plough could tackle it. In the end, a gang of men had to spade it out, working on the 'bench' system, step by step right to the top beyond Halsgrove.

Up on the Room Hill road, just where it starts from Comer's Cross, we had the episode of the Hendon "blower" snow-plough, which was highly amusing and entertaining to us, though not so funny to the men in charge. We had been told that we would be especially honoured by being sent the Hendon Airport plough, which would arrive as soon as it came back south from doing service in Yorkshire, and that this would be set first to clear the main Dulverton–Exford road. The great thing duly arrived one day via Ash Lane, shepherded up to Comer's Cross by the local snow-ploughs etc. We were up at the turnips at the time, and shouldering our spades, went out to see the fun. The monster looked like a diesel train off the rails, and was full of throbbing power. It had been clearing roads like this in Yorkshire at the rate of a mile in three-quarters of an hour, the men said, and added confidently that they would be down in Exford in less than two hours. They then got the thing lined up for the Room Hill stretch, the snow of which was by this time packed down to seven feet of ice. With a roar it was off, whirling blades gnashing, and a stream of pulverized snow-ice streaming from its nose as from a surfacing whale. It proceeded about a hundred yards and then made an even fiercer gnashing sound, and stopped. Slowly it backed out, stood for a while, and then made another start. It proceeded a few yards beyond its first limit, and then came to an abrupt stop again, this time with an ominous clanking sound. Once more it disengaged itself, and backed to the Cross. Something had busted, a man said, and would have to be repaired. They would made a fresh start tomorrow. So we went back to our turnips.

It was in fact several days before the thing got going again, and then by luck we were up there at the time. It roared into life, took aim, and as you might say, took a run at it. It drove right into the packed snow-ice, made a crashing sound, shuddered, and was silent. This time it had embedded itself in the snow, and was helpless. Something had obviously gone in the guts. We walked along to it, and started to dig at the cab doors, as these were jammed in by the snow. "What a blessing she didn't catch on fire," was the comment of the driver as he scrambled out.

What happened to it after that, I don't know. It must have been towed-out ignominiously, and taken back to Hendon with its tail between its legs, so to speak, for we did not see it again. After this the Room Hill road was left to Nature to deal with, as she did in due course. We secretly felt very proud of our snow. It was obviously the real thing, far superior to the sort of stuff they had up in Yorkshire.

The only practical way to clear the roads at this stage was by spading-out, and we had gangs of men sent to us from other parts. I remember a gang slogging away at the Landacre road as I went down to the bridge one day. They told me they had come here from Dartmoor, and that conditions there were nothing like so bad. They had never met snow quite like this before. Again, I could not forbear to feel a secret twinge of triumph.

At long last the snow began to wilt away of its own accord. By April even the biggest drifts were breaking-up, that is all except on the highest ground, where they lay until May. By mid-April hunting was resumed again, after a break of some fifteen weeks. The roads were open, and traffic moved on wheels again. I went to Barnstaple on the bus – the first to cross Exmoor for more than three months. I remember there was still a lot of snow up over the Forest.

The remarkable thing about the thaw when it came, and the blessing we were most thankful for, was that the snow went gradually of its own accord, just freezing and thawing, freezing and thawing, and withering away into the ground. Had we had heavy rain, and a quick thaw, the floods would have been fearful, and this was the thing we dreaded as we turned towards the spring. But fate was merciful, and spared us this upon top of our other tribulations. One hazard, though, we did have to face with the thaw. This was the fall of the hard-packed snow from the roofs, which, with a rush and a rumble, would suddenly come tumbling down into the yards a ton at a time. as "maister" warned us, the strike of it would break the back of a bullock, let along our necks.

Thus we came through the great winter of 1963, and into the days of summer again. Summer it was, almost at once. Everything came together with a rush – snowdrops, primroses and bluebells, all mixed up. Things flourished with a resurgent energy. Lambing was quite good, all things considered. The corn was late going in that year – May 17th at Weatherslade – but made a good crop. The Weatherslade oats harvested in October came up in sheaves as big and heavy as those of Midland wheat.

Some lessons were learnt. One was that in such a crisis the old traditional order of things was best. Those farmers of the "old sort" who managed their stock in the old way, had barns full of hay, and good stocks of other things laid in before Christmas, also wood-burning stoves, and simple plumbing, came through in good order, without trouble, and with very few losses amongst the stock. Those with the most modern ideas were the first to get into difficulties. But that is all by the way, as one may say, for such a winter comes but once in a lifetime. Since then, nothing very extraordinary has happened in or around Withypool, and the seasons come and go without great event. Withypool under the moor is still just itself, and I for one pray that it may always be so.

Last words: As I finish this chapter, snow is starting to fall, and heavily. What I wonder, lies ahead of us?

CHAPTER FOURTEEN

Odds and Ends

Every book should have an odds-and-ends chapter, into which one can push all the things that have not found a place in any other, yet which one feels should be included somewhere.

In writing the preceding chapters I have shown, or tried to show, how much of interest there is packed into one single moorland parish. Landscape and fine scenery, wild-life, sport, agriculture, horticulture, local architecture, archaeology, the historical past – and the prospect of the future – one may spend half a lifetime here ever discovering things of fresh interest, even as one may wander day after day amongst the fields and woods, by the streams and the river and up over the high moor, never wearying of the natural scene, always finding some nook or corner one has not wholly explored before, and marvelling that so much is contained in so small an area of the earth's surface.

Here every day is full, and not one of these days passes without something of interest or note occurring.

One of the commonest – and the stupidest – remarks I so often hear, or overhear, from summer "visitors" is: "... but what do you do here?" Or, with more emphasis, "what do you do in the winter?" Well, one lives.

Just that. Despite the gradually changing pattern of local life – the greater influx of "outsiders" desiring to spend their retirement in this unspoilt corner of the world, and the consequent lessening numbers of "work-a-day" folk – Withypool as a whole is still a purely agricultural parish. There is no other industry, and anybody who is engaged in anything at all (other than our rector, sub-postmaster, and inn-keeper) is engaged in farming in one way or another. And anyone who does this leads a pretty full life, both in terms of physical effort and personal interest. (What do you do in the winter, indeed? Try feeding, watering, and mucking-out forty head of cattle lying-in, taking the feed up to beasts lying-out on distant ground, "looking" sheep in the teeth of the worst possible weather etc. with the dark closing in before one half of what should be done is done, and find out). As to those who fall into the class of the "retired", or "independent", they have gardens, and so are in their way also bound to the land.

Hunting, of which I have already said much, fills the months from August to April, and is the sport of the country. Everybody loves to see the hounds. Hunting is very much the life of the district, and even those of us who have not the means to keep a horse still contrive to get a good day by other means. If one knows the country one can have as good sport on foot as by riding or driving in a Land Rover. Hunting on foot is one of the very best of exercises, both of body and mind. A morning on the Hill, or in the deep tangly combes, scrambling, running, climbing, facing whatever weather the day sends, pitting one's wits and knowledge of the ground against the ways of the wild, is marvellously exhilarating, and sends one home with a ravenous appetite and a deep feeling of satisfaction and well-being (and if hunting on foot depends on knowing the country intimately, in reverse it is hunting on foot that gives one a knowledge of the country in every detail, its every nook, gap, twist and turn, such as one gets by no other means).

As well as hunting, though in lesser degree, there are other field-sports. Fishing of course fills the calendar in due season, and draws visitors to the place. The Barle is the big river of Exmoor, and holds salmon in all of its reaches. Trout fill the smaller streams, and even here the salmon come well up. I have seen some big fish taken out of Pennycombe Water. Fishing, however, is not a subject on which I can discourse at any length, for it is a sport or pastime I know little about, having never been myself a fisherman.

There is rough shooting to be had likewise in due season, mostly of rabbits or hares. Both black and red grouse exist on the moor, but the dreadful winter decimated them to such an extent that they can hardly be regarded as fair game at present. Pheasants and partridges are rare, for the wet climate does not suit them. Mallard are occasional. Wood-pigeons abound however, but ironically few folk seem to think them worth a cartridge, which is a pity, for pigeon-pie is good, and anyway whoever shoots wood-pigeons is a public benefactor – I speak with the heartless feeling of a gardener who has had to endure the depredations of this pest. (Likewise, whoever shoots rabbits is a benefactor – on one occasion rabbits got into my garden and in a single night ate 25 young cauliflowers. Was I mad!) Deer and foxes one does not officially shoot in this country, but there are occasions when one may do so. In general, there is reason and opportunity to have a gun in one's hands at most times of the year. Both shot-gun and rifle have a place here. Myself, I prefer a rifle – a .22 will do for most purposes, and anyway it is difficult to get a permit for a heavier calibre in this district. Shooting like hunting is a sport proper to the country, and I am told that this coming year a clay-pigeon club is to be formed in the Withypool district, to be inaugurated at the Flower Show with a local championship shoot on the Hill at the end of the day.

Falconry has been practised in the district from time to time, though we have no resident falconer here in Withypool. This is a natural country of hawks and the creatures they prey upon, and a region well suited to the sport. Grouse, rooks, and pigeons serve the peregrine, lesser birds the merlin, and rabbits and hares the goshawk. There is no lovelier sight than the bird on the fist – except its flight and stoop. When again shall we see a falconer here on the Hill?

Returning to the river, canoeing seems to be attracting the attention of certain vigorous youngsters from somewhere, for at various times when the water is high, brightly-coloured kayaks may be suddenly espied careering downstream to and through the bridge and away towards Dulverton. Like red, blue, and yellow ducks they bob and weave in the swirling water, miraculously kept upright by the skilled and forceful paddling of their youthful occupants. Such fun it looks, and how I wish I could join them!

In the summer, for those who have the time, there is always the pleasure of just walking. Long walks on summer days, with a picnic out of one's satchel half-way, are amongst the greatest pleasures of this country. To eat out of doors, curled up in a sunny sheltered nook, after vigorous exercise, and with a fine view before one, or the rushing of a stream at one's feet, is a joy in itself. How good food always tastes out of doors! From Withypool a distance of less than a mile in any direction will bring one to as wild and pretty places, or as varied scenery as any in the whole region, whilst a radius of five miles will take one to more distant stretches of Exmoor, and ten to the farther parts of it. Upon one's own feet one can be an explorer of hills, combes, rivers and woods to one's heart's content.

Then, on really hot summer days there is always Sherdon Pool! The pool is that broad stretch of water which lies at, or rather just below, the confluence of Sherdon Water with the River Barle. It is long, wide and deep, free from rocks and offers one of the few really good bathing-places in the valley. Here one can undress amongst the rushes, and then swim or splash or laze to one's heart's content, with the bracken hills nodding to one all around. Only, if it really is a scorching hot day in summer one is unlikely to have it to oneself, for it is well-known locally, and at week-ends is quite a lido, with cars and Land Rovers in attendance on the rough track above.

One of the pleasantest of occupations if one has the time and aptitude, is sketching. With such lovely and varied country all around, and the passing seasons full each with their own rich colouring, every day is an inspiration. Scenes and subjects are endless – the moor with its great skyscapes of towering cloud, the valleys with their trees crowding down to the streams and bending over the water, the pattern of fields with the farmsteads enfolded in the midst, the grazing beasts, the wild things and the birds of the air, the drama and pageant of the hunt. The colour here also is a tremendous stimulation. At all times the colours of nature, from the wild blue skies of spring to the red-gold leaves of autumn, are of greater intensity and brilliance than in any other part of England that I know. This I have observed and noted often, the reasons for this I do not altogether know, but would make a guess that it is caused by the quality of the light deriving from the extreme clarity of the air at most times, and this in turn being due to the high altitude combined with the proximity of the sea. All that I do certainly know is that if I put down on paper the colours as I see them at certain times, then other folk, not used to living with the moor as I do, think that I am exaggerating and making these colours over-brilliant. But this is not so, for it is the one thing I try never to do. The colours are just like that, as near as hand and eye can make them. No-where, except in Australia, have I seen sky of such an electric-blue as I have beheld often enough over the high hills of Exmoor.

As a finale to these few words on sketching, I would warn any prospective Exmoor artist that he or she must be pretty tough and prepared to face wild weather if wishing truly to capture the spirit of the hills, for the best colours and finest scenes are to be had as a rule on the wildest days. To know and record the moor in its heart and spirit one must be about in battering wind and driving rain, or in ice and snow, ready to sit down on the wet ground at the moment when the great clouds rip apart and the glorious light plays on the land for a few moments and then to try to make a hasty record with the wind trying to tear the clamped-down paper from one's board and splatters of rain spoiling what little one can do, and one's fingers becoming numb with the raw cold all the while. It is wonderful though what one can achieve if one is really determined – and anyway, there are fine days as well!

Plant-hunting can offer much interest if one is of a botanical turn of mind, for there are many rare plants, or varieties of plants, or plants peculiar to high moorland country to be found in or around this district. But I would be foolish to name them, or hint at their whereabouts, for once a thing is known it is in danger from those who are either less scrupulous or less careful in the matter of disturbance than they should be.

Bird-watching can be an interesting hobby if one has a pair of field-glasses. As well as the resident moorland birds, there are many migrant and often rare birds-of-passage to be seen at various times. Perhaps as in the case of rare flowers, it is best not to specify the most interesting that may be met with. However, there can be no harm in mentioning what must surely be the most amazing feather visitor ever to descend upon Withypool: a flamingo. This exotic bird appeared "out of the blue" some years ago, haunted the Barle for a few days and then disappeared as mysteriously as it had come. Whether it had been blown from afar off by some great gale, or had escaped from a less distant private zoo, was never ascertained.

Gardening, of course is all-absorbing, both of time and interest. One can spend a lifetime just pottering in one's own garden and watching things grow. Then there is the weather. The weather is always uncertain and variable and a subject of great interest. Much conversation revolves around the weather, which to us all, we being either farmers or gardeners, is a matter of prime importance.

One can hold long discussions upon the weather. The latter being on the whole quite unpredictable and seemingly unanswerable to any scientific methods of forecasting, it is up to anyone to be a weather-prophet according to their means. Older inhabitants recall experiences of their youth, and compare or co-relate these to present times. Next after snow it is rain that is to be chiefly noted. Our annual rainfall is a high one, averaging some 60 inches a year and liable to be at its worst when it is least wanted – i.e. at lambing and haymaking etc. Sometimes it comes in torrential downpours and sometimes in showers of a frequency which never lets anything dry up for weeks – perhaps months – on end. Then there are days of the insidious 'misty wet' when a fine driving rain penetrates everything everywhere and permeates everything with damp and causes fungi and mould to sprout indoors and out. Then when the water-table gets too high and the sponge of the soil too sopping-wet to hold any more moisture, little forgotten springs and run-off courses suddenly break into life in top gardens, back-yards, and best parlours, and send swilling water into houses and out again to go down the hill to join the spilling streams. ("Did you have the water in last night?" is one of the polite questions one asks of one's neighbours after heavy prolonged rain). Then too, coupled with the misty-wet are the days of hill-fog, when the white hill-mist blots out all distances and one cannot see more than a few paces ahead of one, and all things are ghostly, and to venture on the moor away from any known track is to be lost at once. Gales and storms, frequent enough in this hill-country near the sea, are likewise subjects for comment and reminiscence. The sou'west wind, rain-laden, comes only too often tearing across the land, ripping slates and snapping branches, battering everything and roaring with deafening voice in all the beech-hedges. Violent thunderstorms, often accompanied by vicious hail, strike the hills from time, and then the lightning stabs all around, attracted by the iron in the rocks. Both sheep and cattle may be struck, and again one enquires of one's neighbours upon next meeting if all is well with them. But if bad days are to be noted, so also are good ones. The first lovely days of spring when one feels the earth stirring from under the blanket of winter, the long hot ones of midsummer when even the beasts seek the shade under the hedges heavy with leaf, the autumn mornings when the golden sun pierces the early mist for a cloudless day that may be hotter than August, the fair days that may come in the midst of winter like a benediction to the land – these too are events of note.

Then there is the weekly advent of the *Free Press*. This official organ of news, our "local rag", is the *West Somerset Free Press*, and it comes into the village on Saturday mornings. It tells us everything we want to know, and the things we want to know most in great detail. Its front page is devoted to the announcement of sales and auctions, one of its inner pages to hunting – giving at length the reports of at least five packs of hounds and the appointments of as many as ten or twelve – and the rest of its sheets collectively to market-prices, flower shows, horse shows, local football and racing, council meetings, weddings, funerals, police court proceedings, things wanted or for sale, advertisements of all sorts, and, sandwiched somewhere between the foregoing, interesting notes on history, archaeology, and wildlife. Altogether, it is an indispensable 7d-worth.

Daily life in general is punctuated by the fortnightly arrival of the County Library van, which comes lurching along the narrow lane every second Monday, to draw up at half-past three in the afternoon just opposite the Post Office. What a wonderful service this is! Our van, whose headquarters is at Minehead, carries a thousand books at a time, on every subject under the sun, and not only does it come into the village, but makes the round of the loneliest farms, so bringing good reading where it is most needed. (A propos of this, when the service was first started, the van had many adventures, cracking its springs over stones, getting stuck in the mud or in the fords, and coming to abrupt conclusions with tractors and bullocks, from which encounters it emerged with honourable scars. Sometimes its adventures put it out of action for periods of time, but always it managed to get repaired in the end. Needless to say, our librarian has always had to combine the qualities of literary scholarship with the driving-abilities of a cross-country trials-driver). And what a marvellous thing it is to step inside this library-on-wheels, having perhaps waited (as I have often done) huddled under a hedge in the pouring driving rain at some lonely spot on the edge of the moor, and there be confronted by the ranged shelves or brightly-jacketed books all offering themselves for the taking! No Aladdin's cave was ever more wonderful or more entrancing. Here the whole world comes to one between the covers of books. The return journey with the precious books held tightly under the raincoat is like the bearing of treasure, and the weight a happy one, foretelling a cosy evening of reading and looking at pictures. (How well I remember the mornings at Higher Blackland when the farming day began with the words: "It's Library day today," and time was made amongst the chores for the journey out to Bradymoor Gate – Blackland being one of the farms to which the van did not go directly, the lane in those days being very rough indeed).

Another fortnightly occurrence to be remembered is what is called in the elegant local phrasing "Dirt Day". In other words the local refuse-collection. Yes, we actually get a council collection. (Prior to this an annual or twice-yearly personal trip to a handy quarry-pit did service). It is an important affair, involving a shifting of bins etc. down to road gates.

Church marks the Sundays for the faithful – the little chapel is now closed down – but the services are variable, having to be held in conjunction with those of Hawkridge. It is necessary to check from the church-gate notice-board.

The mail comes into the Post Office at seven o'clock in the morning, and the delivery-round starts at half-past seven. Waiting for the postman is one of the anticipations of the day, and the picking up of letters a moment of excitement – for me at least.

Of the Post Office itself I have already spoken. It is the hub of daily life, and the supplier of all our wants and needs. Hard by is the parish noticeboard, which is always worth a look, just in case anything extraordinary is pending, such as the changing of the Dirt Days or a local election.

Sales and auctions are important events which are social occasions as well as necessary business functions. They fall into two categories: market auctions and property sales. The former, particularly those of the autumn months are of the greatest general importance to all for upon them and their prices depends the livelihood of the hill-farmers. But, in true West Country tradition they also provide a day out, with the opportunity of meeting friends and relatives, and eating and drinking and gossiping, and fixing future affairs. The chief auction yards for our district are Exford (sheep) and Cutcombe (sheep and cattle) though some folk take their stock to Raleigh's Cross on the Brendons or Blackmoor Gate over in North Devon. There is also South Molton and for ponies, Bampton Fair at the end of October. Property sales are of course of importance principally to the person selling-out, but everybody goes to them regardless of whether they intend to buy or not. Again, it is a day out with the possibility of a bargain thrown in. Once, it was the custom for the vendor to entertain all helpers and bona-fide buyers with substantial refreshment in barn or kitchen, but in these harder times a mobile canteen van usually has to do duty. Most people still contrive to enjoy themselves, anyway.

In the evenings there is the wireless and the "telly", for we now have main-electricity in the village. It came a few years ago, and on the whole the job was very well done, with the poles sited as inconspicuously as possible. Most households have the 'phone – which to the isolated farms is a boon and a blessing – and so folk can ring up and have a chat on a dark night if they are lonely. So you see, we have all "mod cons" and daily interest.

Of annual festivals and events we have several. The Flower Show (already described at length), the Harvest Festival, St Andrew's Feast, the Christmas Carol Service, the closing meeting of the Staghounds at Comer's Gate, and in August, just beyond the bounds of the parish, upon Room Hill, the Exford Horse Show. Then, further afield, the various race-meetings in due season.

Of the purely local events, the Harvest Festival probably ranks next in importance to the Flower Show. What a joyous occasion it is for the little church! The occasion usually takes place on a Friday evening in October, just about dusk, and one approaches the porch, with the church lights radiant through the open door. Within, the place is full, both of humanity and the fruits of the earth. The windowsills are banked with glowing autumn flowers and every nook and corner is filled with vegetables piled up in splendour. Oat-sheaves recline against the font and tufts of oats nod from the warden's staves. Wool too is laid as an offering upon the floor, for fleeces are our harvest here even more than the oaten sheaves. Upon the altar and behind it and amongst the flowers on the windowsills the many candles gleam like stars, more beautiful than all the electric lights that look downwards from the roof to illuminate the body of the church. The organ mutters and grows in strength and the ancient hymns ring out again with what vigour and enthusiasm they are sung! "We plough the fields and scatter ...", "Come ye thankful people come ...", "To thee O Lord our hearts we raise ...", these and their words, like the Psalms, have here a meaning and a truth which is lacking in a more urban society. The children peep through their fingers, for our Rector is resplendent this festive day in a cope of gorgeous yellow silk set off with a sky-blue hood. At last comes the blessing, and we turn out through the porch laden with turnips and onions into the now-dark – and usually wet – night to go down the road and up the hill to the harvest supper in the village hall. Here is bright light again and festivity of another sort. Down the long room is a table laden with delicacies of all sorts, and all around willing helpers. The Rector says grace, then we all eat and drink and talk and talk. Then, when all have had their fill, the table is cleared and the cards brought out, and we settle down to an evening of that greatly loved game, whist. It is late and very dark indeed when we at length stumble out of the brilliantly-lighted room into the night. Another Harvest Home over, another landmark in the year passed by – soon the next thing will be Christmas and the church will be filled with holly and fir. But in between will come St Andrew's Feast on 30th November. This festival is similar in its special service, tea, and card-party to the Harvest celebration but is more a purely church occasion than the Harvest Festival, the latter being in the nature of a general Thanksgiving to which all parishioners go irrespective of their religious denomination.

For those who can get into Dulverton, our local township nine miles away, there are such activities as an Art Group, a Camera Club, a Drama Society, and all sorts of other things.

So you see, life is not dull. One thing only do we lack in this present day and age, and that is a bus service of any sort. This is a deprivation, for though the "Powers that Be" go on the assumption that everybody in these days has a car, as a matter of fact everybody hasn't, and for the have-nots it is very difficult to get anywhere beyond walking distance. Though in the ordinary way folk like me have no desire to go far, yet there are some times when it is necessary to do so, and then it is a real problem, for no-one in the village does taxi-service any more, and one shrinks from bothering one's friends.

When one is not actually engaged in one or other of these activities, one talks about them. Gossip is a local pastime in itself. One of the nice things about Withypool is the sense of community which still exists. Here there is no such thing as loneliness. Everybody knows everybody, and everyone is a neighbour. In daily life conversation flows easily, running on and revolving round every possible topic from farming problems to political matters – pride of place usually being taken by the iniquities of the weather. In time of trouble help is always at hand. Many centuries of hard moorland life has bred kind hearts and a sense of fellowship. Even newcomers are caught into this stream of immemorial life, and the local ways and customs perpetuated. May it ever remain so.

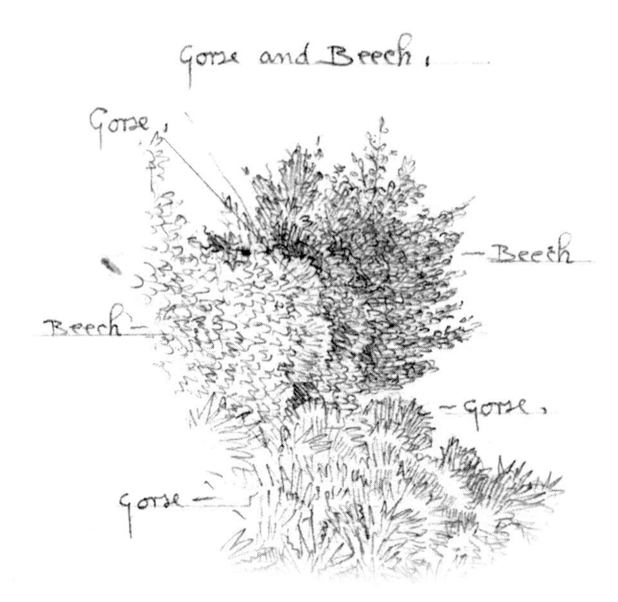

Appendix

The fifty-two free suits of Withypool and Hawkridge according to the two surviving lists of 1797 and 1819

Withypool 1797

Tenements	Suits
South Batsham	1
North Batsham	1
Blackmoreland	1
South Hill	1
Kings	1
Waterhouse	1
Knighton	2
Brightonworthy	4
Landacre	4
Hillway	2
Blackland	3
Woolpitland	1
Halsgrove	1
Foxtwitchen	1
Witherslade	1
Sweetwalls	1
Uppington	1
Garliscombe	1
Dodhays	1

Withypool 1819

Tenements	Suits
Higher Lanacre	2
Lower Lanacre	2
Hillway	2
Hole or Hawlse	1
East Hole	1
Higher Blackland	2
Lower Blackland	1
Woolpit Land	1
Newland	3
Higher Brightworthy	1 ½
Middle Brightworthy	1 ½
Lower Brightworthy	1
Knighton	2
Waterhouse	1
Broadmead	1
Halsgrove	1
Weatherslade	1
Foxtwitchen	1
Dadhays	1

Wayhouse	1
Broadmeadhouse	1
Gibbs	1
Hole	2
Newland	3

Gibbs	1
Garliscombe (mill)	1
Wayhouse	1
Sweetwalls	1
Kings	1
Uppington	1
South Hill	1
Blackmoreland	1
North Batsham	1
South Batsham	1

Hawkridge 1797

Tenements	Suits
Ham	2
E. Rew	1
Wilskier	1
Kelskier	1
Holecombe	1
W. Holecombe	1
Colland	1
Slade	1
Sayles	2
Shortcombeland	2
Foxcombe	1
Huntercombly	1
	52

Hawkridge 1819

Tenements	Suits
Ham and Putsham	2
Huntercombe Ley	1
Foxcombe	1
Shorcombe	1
Wester Shorcombe	1
Wester Sayles	1
Easter Sayles	1
Slade	1
West Hollacombe	1
East Hollacombe	1
East Rew	1
Kelshire or Colsher	1
Wilshire	1
Collands	1
	52

A careful comparison of these two lists will show that they are in fact identical, despite what would at first sight seem to be some discrepancy. The greater number of named holdings upon the 1819 list is due to a more precise definition of the attachment of suits. (This latter list was drawn up in connection with the Enclosure Awards following the disafforestation of Exmoor, and so had to be as detailed as possible). The more condensed version of 1797 appears so because of the amalgamation – temporary or permanent – of certain of the holdings, and its simple purpose was that of defining what suit each holder should give. For practical purposes this older list is the more sensible, because for each suit a man on horseback had to be present. Half a horseman would have been difficult to produce!

It follows that the holdings with the more numerous suits are the larger farms. If, as is my guess, each suit once upon a time represented a single holding or tenement, then one must look about the land of any farm with two or more suits for the remains of some now long-forgotten homestead which has been absorbed by the former. Take for instance Blackland. There are two farms there, Higher and Lower, but the collective suit is three. So one wonders if there were ever a third farmstead. Now, on looking round the sunny slopes of Blackland Ball, one comes across a tiny broken-banked enclosure like a small yard in an angle amongst the bigger hedges. It is right in the eye of the sun, with the ball of the hill falling away to the encircling streams just below. This nook intrigued me right from the first, and I asked if there had ever been a building here. No-one could remember such ever existing here, however, nor offer any explanation for the tiny plat. Then, when a short while ago I saw the old tithe map for the first time, I noticed that there was indeed a building marked at this spot. Just the black rectangle of a farm outbuilding, but enough to set me thinking again. It was, and is, my feeling that here was once a dwelling too, and that this was long ago a tiny holding constituting the third part of Blackland. Of course this is only guesswork, but looking across to the Ball from Kitridge Lane, this spot strikes one as being just such as site as some long-ago settler would choose.

The tracing of the origin of the fifty-two suits would make an intriguing subject for anyone sufficiently interested in local history.

With regard to the identification of the named tenements, those of Withypool are fairly easily traced. The larger farms still exist as such today. Broadmead and Wayhouse remain as private houses. Sweetwalls, Garliscombe, Woolpits, and South Batsham are still remembered in name, though they have "gone down". The two or three recorded as Gibbs and Hole or Hawlse, would seem to have been very small places set somewhere along the lane that runs from just past the church to Newland. Probably they or their sites are represented by one or other of the dwellings that lie along there. The footpath that runs up from the school to Kitridge Lane is still known locally as "Gibbs".

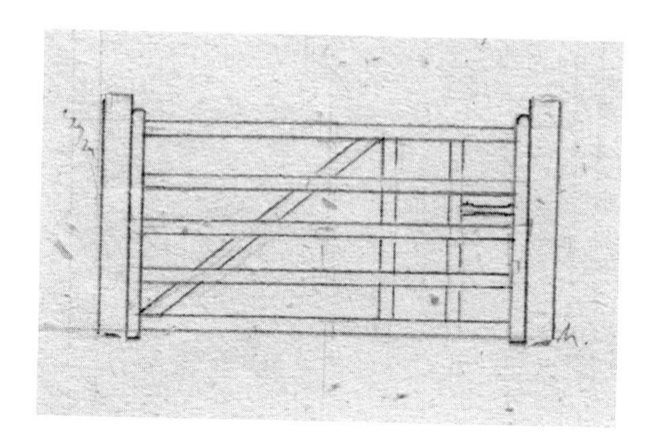